8   BOILED COTTAGE HAM, Whipped Potatoes, Buttered Cabbage   1 10

Roll or Home Made Bread with Butter or Jelly

Choice of Any 15c. Dessert

Coffee, Tea or Milk

Desserts

(Whipped Cream a la Carte - 10c.)

PIES 15:
Lemon Meringue   Fresh Apple   Cocoanut Custard   15
Pineapple-Cheese   Cherry   15

De Luxe Chocolate Layer Cake   Cocoanut Layer Cake   15
Chocolate Whipped Cream Pie   20   Glace Cake   10
Banana Shortcake   20   Peach Halves   15
Hot Apple Pie with Vanilla Sauce   15   Diced Gelatin
Rice Custard Pudding   10   Cup Custard with Cherry Fi...
Apple Sauce Cake, Whipped Cream   20   Fresh Grapefruit Half
French Cheese Cake   15   Fresh Apple Sauce
Fresh Fruit Salad   15

Chocolate Whipped Cream Layer Cake
Baked Apple   20   with Whipped Cream
Glazed Apples   10   with Whipped Cream
Ice Cream with Hot Chocolate Fudge, Maple Nut or Cherry Sauce
ICE CREAM (Our Own Make) Chocolate, Vanilla or Strawberry

(Ice Cream Served with Dessert, 10c. Additional)

Nicola D'Ascenzo's stained glass, Philadelphia.

The AUTOMAT

Lorraine B. Diehl and Marianne Hardart

CLARKSON POTTER/PUBLISHERS

NEW YORK

See page 128 for photograph credits.

Published by Clarkson Potter/Publishers, New York,
New York. Member of the Crown Publishing Group,
a division of Random House, Inc.
www.randomhouse.com

CLARKSON N. POTTER is a trademark and
POTTER and colophon are registered trademarks
of Random House, Inc.

Printed in Singapore

Design by Jan Derevjanik

Library of Congress Cataloging-in-Publication Data

Diehl, Lorraine B.
The automat: the history, recipes, and allure of
Horn & Hardart's masterpiece/Lorraine B. Diehl
and Marianne Hardart.—1st ed.
Includes bibliographical references and index.
1. Vending machines.   I. Hardart, Marianne.
II. Title.
TJ1560 .D54 2002
647.9573—dc21   2001057805

ISBN 0-609-61074-0

10 9 8 7 6 5 4 3 2

First Edition

PASTRIES

For Lizzie

L.B.D.

For my father,
Augustin S. Hardart Jr.

M.H.

CONTENTS

Edward Hopper, *Automat*, 1927. Des Moines Art Center Permanent Collections.

The Automat

Oh, how I love the Automat,

The place where all the food is at!

I like to watch the milk run out

And join the coffee at the spout.

I put a nickel in the slot

And watch to see what I have got.

The little door then opens wide

And gives me what has been inside.

There's cakes and sandwiches galore

And pies and cooked things by the score.

Oh, yes! I love the Automat,

The place where all the food is at.

ELIZABETH M. KOEHNLINE,

Life Magazine, 1938

INTRODUCTION

Mention Horn & Hardart or the Automat to anyone who visited one, and you'll find yourself captivated by a flood of memories, all mouthwatering and wonderful. If you never walked into one of the eighty-four palaces in New York and Philadelphia, you missed out on a unique slice of American history.

First, there was the food: coconut cream and pumpkin pies, vanilla ice cream flecked with real vanilla beans, rice pudding laced with plump raisins. And where else could you get a slice of berry-bursting huckleberry pie? These rewards followed velvety macaroni and cheese, bubbly chicken potpie, or succulent Salisbury steak with the fluffiest mashed potatoes. The creamed spinach was another favorite, along with those unforgettable baked beans. All washed down with a cup of unbeatable "gilt-edged" coffee poured from those famous dolphin-head spouts. It was top-quality comfort food, and every child of the Automat had a favorite.

Cofounder Joe Horn understood the importance of food that lingered in the memory while not emptying the wallets of the working people to whom the Automat catered. The other cofounder, Frank Hardart, brought to the partnership his "secret recipe" for coffee—for thirty-eight years, a cup of Horn & Hardart's coffee cost a nickel. "There is no trick to selling a poor item cheaply," said Horn. "The real trick is to sell a good item cheaply." To make sure the food was consistently up to standard, Horn introduced the Sample Table—one in Philadelphia, another in New York—where every morning, company VIPs tasted forkfuls from among the four hundred menu items prepared twice daily by the commissaries. Standards were high for Horn, whose enormous appetite was legendary. One morning, a thousand gallons of soup were rejected for lacking a single ingredient.

At the Sample Table, from left around the table: engineer John Fritsche, president Joseph Horn (at the head), employees Charles Anderson and Adam Amend, secretary-treasurer Frank Hardart Sr., and John Anderson. Opposite: A directory of Automats in New York City.

But to linger over Horn & Hardart's dishes is to see just half the picture. Every kid who longed for autonomy had his dreams come true at the Automat. A fistful of nickels, thrust across a marble slab by one of the quicker-than-the-eye cashiers known as "nickel throwers," would open the little windows to casseroles, pies, sandwiches, whatever took one's fancy. That famous wall of windows, a mechanical marvel in a country where the pinball machine was yet to make the scene, made the Automat unique.

Neil Simon remembered Depression days when his unemployed mother scraped enough money together to treat him to Sunday-night dinners at the Automat. "To have your own stack of nickels placed in your own tiny hands; to be able to choose your own food, richly on display like museum pieces; to make quick and final decisions at the age of eight, was a lesson in financial dealings that not even two years at the Wharton School could buy today."

For grown-up New Yorkers and Philadelphians, Horn & Hardart was an indelible part of the cityscape, as much a fixture as the corner newsstand and the local movie house. In addition to the famous wall of automatic glass windows, there was a long steam table where hearty stews, moist fish cakes, baked ham, and that wonderful Salisbury steak were served up on heated plates. Busy New Yorkers gravitated to the automatic windows, where they could quickly feed the slots and find sandwiches and crocks of macaroni and cheese. The more leisurely paced citizens of the City of Brotherly Love preferred to eat cafeteria-style; if the ever-present serving lines at the steam table were too long, they could be served by incredibly efficient waitresses with their arms lined with plates.

For both cities, the Automat belonged to everyone. Rich and poor, famous and common, tourists and locals—they all came here. In Philadelphia, it saved many a worker from brown-bag lunches. In New York City, out-of-work actors nursed nickel cups of coffee or tomato soup concocted from catsup and hot water. During his lean days as a student in the 1930s, choreographer Jerome Robbins depended on the Automat—"I had the same lunch every day: three vegetables, a roll, and cocoa. All for twenty-five cents." In Philadelphia, before his *American Bandstand* days, Dick Clark lived on Horn & Hardart's hot chocolate and chicken potpie while saving up to get married. Jazz Age New York mayor Jimmy Walker, who often attended several banquets in one evening, said, "I wish someone would throw one where I'd feel at home: at the Automat."

In Manhattan, each Automat had its own crowd: Horse players liked West Seventy-second Street; Union Square, on the fringe of Greenwich Village, was popular with social activists. Uptown at Columbus, the cabaret crowd gathered in the early-morning hours. Dancers and singers from nearby Carnegie Hall unwound at the Fifty-seventh Street Automat.

In Philadelphia, dock workers hung out at the Horn & Hardart at 234 Market Street, which stayed open around the clock to accommodate their erratic hours.

Jeweler Row diamond merchants did business at the 818 Chestnut Street Automat, while insurance salesmen liked the upstairs tables at 6006 Market Street. And if you wanted the ear of your local politician, you would likely find him at 1508 Market Street, rubbing shoulders with gangsters, who also claimed this Horn & Hardart as their turf.

During its heyday, from the 1920s through the late 1950s, the Automat wove itself into the fabric of the neighborhood and the nation. Irving Berlin celebrated it in song, Hollywood made it a plot device. Comedian Jack Benny, whose shtick was his cheapness, inaugurated his television series with a party at the Automat, presenting each guest with a roll of nickels. On Broadway that wall of windows was reproduced for *Face the Music,* a 1932 show about the Depression, when Horn & Hardart came into its own, as a nickel cup of coffee and a ten-cent piece of pie became very appealing.

The story of the Automat is as much about a time as it is about a place. We were a different country: formal in our manners and dress, but more relaxed about eating meals across from a stranger. We expected more bang for the buck, and we got it. In the 1920s and 1930s, you could eat a full meal for less than fifty cents. In the 1940s and 1950s, a handful of change got you into a double feature with a newsreel and a cartoon. At the Automat, nickels got you what dollars buy today. Of course, there was much more than value: The Automat gave us a taste of who we were and where we were heading.

Part of the original Automat in Philadelphia,
now at the Smithsonian Institution.

Mr. Horn,
meet
Mr. Hardart

There were two things that Joe Horn loved: food and Philadelphia. No problem in the life of the young man—including long days in the family surgical-appliance factory—was so big it couldn't be diminished by a good meal. And no city compared with his beloved Philadelphia. But he didn't learn that until he had crossed the country by railroad.

Opposite: The first Horn & Hardart lunchroom on Thirteenth Street, Philadelphia, 1888. Above: The board of directors.

The journey came about because of Joe's love of food. Sitting around the family dining room table one night, young Joe was pestering his two older brothers about joining them in the restaurant they had opened on Market Street. He did this with such regularity that his exasperated siblings pleaded with their mother to get her youngest child a restaurant of his own. What better way to burst his balloon, they decided, than to let him see for himself how difficult it was to run a restaurant?

Horn's mother was a widow who had raised her seven children on the profits from her late husband's factory; she had no intention of throwing away her money. There would be no restaurant for Joe Horn. Instead, she would send him on a trip, one that would take him to the Pacific Coast, with many stops along the way, where he would hopefully discover another business to claim his interest.

But when the twenty-seven-year-old Horn returned to Philadelphia, the only thing he could talk about were the restaurants he had visited. His mother decided that she hadn't taken a firm enough hand in directing her youngest son, so she sent him away again, this time to Boston with a list of businesses for him to look into. One afternoon, a hungry Joe Horn dropped into Thompson's Spa, a popular restaurant catering to working people whose demands were simple: a good meal delivered quickly. It was in this noisy, bustling place, without a trace of elegance, that Joe discovered his heart's desire: to open a restaurant like Thompson's Spa in Philadelphia.

In 1888, a thousand dollars was a daunting sum of money, especially when placed in the bank account of a young man who hadn't the foggiest idea what he should do with it. It was one thing to convince his mother to give in and stake him in a restaurant. It was quite another to figure out how to put the money to use. As much as Joe Horn loved restaurants, it never occurred to him that he hadn't a clue about running one.

Frank Hardart didn't have that problem. No one in the family of the tall, thin, thirty-eight-year-old man could have given him ten dollars, much less a thousand, to start his own business. Like Joe Horn, he was raised by a widowed mother, but that is all they had in common. Frank Hardart was eight years old when he emigrated to America in 1858 with his mother, two sisters, and his older brother, Philip. The fatherless family was too poor to travel to an area where a heavy German-American population could help them assimilate, so the Bavarian-born Hardarts settled in New Orleans, the city in which their boat had docked.

Life was a constant struggle, with most of the family's income coming from Philip's truck farm, where vegetables were grown and brought to market. At thirteen, young Frank took a job as a dishwasher at a lunch counter in a shabby restaurant in the city's French Quarter; the pay was three dollars a week. The owner rarely showed up for work, so washing dishes was only one part of Frank's long day. He would open up in the morning and close the place at night; he cooked, served food, and acted as cashier. And he was given one more task that, unbeknownst to the overworked boy, would one day help to make him a rich man: Each day, Frank Hardart roasted and ground the coffee, taking great pride in brewing it well. Even in a run-down luncheonette, the citizens of New Orleans expected first-rate coffee. Unlike the rest of the country's coffee, which was boiled and sometimes clarified with egg shells, New Orleans coffee was brewed by the French-drip method, ensuring a mellow flavor with no bitterness.

At twenty, Frank Hardart was working in a different restaurant, this time on St. Charles Street, earning ten dollars a week, when he noticed something: Customers arriving for lunch would often be cranky, and it wasn't until they had their first few sips of coffee that their spirits would lift and their moods soften. Since only those privileged to live in New Orleans had the luxury of good French-drip coffee, why not take that coffee to the rest of the country and allow everyone else to enjoy the same experience?

The Centennial Exhibition of 1876 was being held in Philadelphia, and restau-

rants were humming with out-of-town visitors. With just enough money for a one-way rail ticket, Hardart decided to take his talent to that city and try his luck. After taking a dishwasher job, he attempted to introduce the owner to the New Orleans way of brewing coffee. But the busy man had no time for him. Hardart fared no better in other restaurants. Most of the customers he encountered were creatures of habit: Having known only the taste of boiled coffee, they were quite content to drink more of the same.

Hardart returned to New Orleans, poor but undaunted. For ten years, he thought about little else other than going back to Philadelphia. Timing, he decided, had been his only problem. All he needed was one more shot at the City of Brotherly Love, and they would all be drinking his coffee. Year after year, he scraped and saved. He found a wife—a young Irishwoman named Mary Bruen—who believed in his dream enough to scrape and save along with him. When they finally arrived in Philadelphia in 1886, there was little for Mary to hold on to but her husband's dreams.

There were more restaurant jobs—two years of them, waiting on tables for small wages—with little else to sustain the couple but Frank Hardart's now-threadbare dream. He was invited to become a partner in a New Jersey soda fountain, but no sooner had it gotten off the ground when cold weather marked its end. The thirty-eight-year-old Hardart finally settled into a job at a place called Joe Smith's, a luncheonette in a run-down section of Philadelphia. It looked as if his dream to bring a good cup of coffee to the citizens of Philadelphia would remain precisely that.

In another part of town, though, Joe Horn was trying to breathe life into *his* dream. He knew he couldn't afford to squander the thousand dollars his mother had advanced him; this was his only chance, and he had to make it work. He decided that he needed a partner, someone who knew the nuts and bolts of the restaurant business. In 1888, the twenty-seven-year-old entrepreneur placed an ad in a local newspaper, and waited. There were no replies. Finally, one arrived from someone with a rooming-house address. There was no formal letter, only a torn-off remnant from a sugar bag. On it were written three words: "I'm your man." It was signed F. Hardart.

The new partners, each desperate for success, were not about to allow any moss to grow beneath their feet. They immediately went about scouring the streets of Philadelphia for a suitable property, finally coming upon a tiny, eleven-by-seventeen-foot lunchroom at 39 South Thirteenth Street, opposite Wanamaker's Department Store. On December 22, 1888, three days before Christmas, the first Horn & Hardart restaurant opened. There were no tables, just a counter long enough to accommodate fifteen stools. On the window were the names J. HORN, F. HARDART.

Joe Horn served and Frank Hardart worked in the kitchen, preparing the food and finally brewing the French-drip coffee that earned immediate praise. "You have the best cup of coffee in town," one first-day customer said, a comment that would hold the same sacred place between the partners as a first earned dollar bill. Days before their grand opening, the enterprising duo had done a bit of self-promotion,

Horn & Hardart was always clean, never dirty. You'd look through those little windows and see all the food already prepared. It was a showcase.

BARBARA BUSCAGLIA,
Secretary

dropping off business cards in prominent areas of town, letting everyone know that genuine New Orleans coffee had arrived in Philadelphia. This delicious "gilt-edge" brew—a term Hardart coined for his French-drip coffee—would be the anchor for a venture that was brimming with ambition.

This was a heady time for the new partners. Even with the paltry sum of $7.25 in the cash register at the end of their first day, they both knew they had the desire, focus, and talent to make it a success. In fact, as news of the luncheonette's great coffee spread, more customers came until it was standing-room-only at lunch. Horn, the young man who always wanted to own a restaurant in his native Philadelphia, was finally living his dream. For the hardworking Hardart, this tiny luncheonette marked the end of his poverty-ridden days eking out a living as a dishwasher and waiter.

Hardart took great pride in his cooking, and Horn maintained Olympian standards of quality. Before long, more lunchrooms owned by the partners began popping up around town. From the beginning, the partners were keenly aware of pleasing their customers. In a 1934 *New York Evening Journal* article, Clarence E. Heller described his encounter with Frank Hardart in that first restaurant: "I can still see him in the tiny, vest-pocket edition restaurant, grasping hands of customers he knew, asking them how things were, inviting them back."

To keep costs down, a central commissary was built at 202–210 South Tenth Street, where the food for all the restaurants was baked and prepared. Years later, the commissary concept made it possible for Joe Horn to maintain his exacting standards in 165 locations—Automats, cafeterias, and retail food shops in two major cities. By 1898, the partnership that had been sealed with nothing more than a handshake was incorporated, becoming the Horn & Hardart Baking Co., with thirty-seven-year-old Joe Horn as president and forty-eight-year-old Frank Hardart as secretary-treasurer. And then a third man entered the picture. His name is unknown and unimportant, but what he was selling would soon change the dining habits of Philadelphians and New Yorkers.

The one near us was at Fifty-fourth and City Line in Philadelphia. My family went to Horn & Hardart whenever we went out to eat. One day, I was reading a Frank Brookhouser column. He was the Man About Town. He said something about not having brought a dinner jacket somewhere and he had to go and eat in a Horn & Hardart. The scales fell off my eyes. That was the first time I ever knew that Horn & Hardart was not an elegant restaurant.

DEBORAH HARKINS, Writer, *New York Daily News*

Creamed Spinach

serves 4

1 pound spinach, washed well and drained but not dried
2 tablespoons unsalted butter
1½ tablespoons flour
¼ cup milk
1 teaspoon sugar
¼ teaspoon salt, plus more to taste
¼ teaspoon white pepper, plus more to taste

Add the spinach to a large pan over medium heat and cook, covered, until thoroughly wilted, about 5 minutes. Remove from heat, let cool, and chop finely. Set aside.

Meanwhile, melt the butter in a medium saucepan over low heat. Add the flour gradually, whisking constantly, and cook 1 to 2 minutes, or until a smooth mixture forms. Continue to whisk and gradually add the milk; cook 3 to 5 minutes, until thickened. Add the reserved spinach and the salt and pepper, and blend well. Season to taste with additional salt and pepper.

Cup Custard

serves 8

1 quart milk
½ cup sugar
2 teaspoons vanilla extract
6 large eggs

Preheat the oven to 325°F.

In a medium bowl, combine the milk, sugar, and vanilla, and mix well. In a large bowl, whisk the eggs until well beaten. Stirring constantly, gradually add the milk mixture to the eggs. Divide evenly among 8 custard cups.

Place the custard cups in a $13 \times 9 \times 2$ baking pan; fill the pan with hot water to come halfway up the sides of the custard cups. Bake in the preheated oven 40 to 45 minutes, until a knife inserted in the center of the custard comes out clean. Remove the cups from the water and let stand at room temperature about 20 minutes. Cover and refrigerate until chilled, about 2 hours.

Baked Beans

serves 8 to 10

1 pound dried navy beans, rinsed

1 large yellow onion, chopped (about 1 cup)

4 slices bacon, diced

2 tablespoons sugar

1 tablespoon dry mustard

¼ teaspoon cayenne pepper

⅔ cup molasses

2 tablespoons cider vinegar

1½ cups tomato juice

Salt to taste

Place the beans in a large saucepot and cover with cold water. Let stand overnight at room temperature. Drain, place in an 8-quart saucepot, add fresh water to cover, and bring to a boil. Reduce the heat to low and simmer, uncovered, until the beans are almost tender, 45 minutes to 1 hour. Drain, reserving 1 cup of the cooking liquid.

Preheat the oven to 250°F.

Return the beans with the other ingredients and the 1 cup reserved cooking liquid to the pot; mix to combine. Pour into a 9 × 13 × 2 baking pan or a Dutch oven. Bake, uncovered, until very tender, approximately 4 hours. Check the beans occasionally while baking and add water if necessary to prevent the mixture from drying out. Season with salt and let cool 5 to 10 minutes before serving.

Pumpkin Pie

serves 8

2 cups cooked pumpkin (one 15-ounce can)

¾ teaspoon salt

1 14½-ounce can evaporated milk

2 large eggs

¾ cup sugar

1 tablespoon unsalted butter

1 teaspoon ground cinnamon

¼ teaspoon ground ginger

¼ teaspoon ground nutmeg

1 11-inch prepared pastry crust

Preheat oven to 425°F.

In a large bowl, beat together all the ingredients (except the crust) with a rotary beater or hand whisk until the mixture is smooth. Line an 11-inch pie tin with the pastry. Pour in the filling, and bake in the preheated oven for 40 minutes, or until a knife inserted in the center of the pie comes out clean.

Oh, be still my heart! I used to shine shoes when I was fourteen years old. And when I was a little ahead, I would stop at Horn & Hardart. The pumpkin pie was delicious.

TONY CURTIS

Acentury was ending and another about to begin, one that was anxious to leave the sensibilities of the 1800s to history books and museums. The salesman who approached Joe Horn and Frank Hardart was offering a product that would serve the modern, faster-paced society that marked the new twentieth century splendidly. The salesman had been having trouble convincing potential clients—New Yorkers in particular—that his revolutionary gadget would fit their new lifestyles. He decided to try his luck in Philadelphia, where he had heard of two enterprising men who might be open to new ideas.

Opposite: Elegant interior of the Times Square Automat, 1912. Above: An early postcard.

His product was a Swiss invention, with a prototype manufactured in Germany, and it served food—sandwiches, chocolate bars, and wine—automatically. It was known as the "waiterless restaurant," or simply the "automatic." All the salesman had were drawings and plans; the actual machine was on the other side of the ocean. But Frank Hardart had never had a proper vacation, so he decided he'd go to Germany and give this new contraption the once-over. Automatic or waiterless restaurants were not uncommon in Europe, particularly in Germany and Scandinavia, although their scale was much more modest than what their future held in America. When Hardart saw the machine, he was not merely intrigued—it was love at first sight. With no hesitation, he parted with thirty thousand dollars to have one made and shipped to Philadelphia.

It took the Quisisana Company a year to manufacture the machine. In 1901, it was shipped to Liverpool and transferred to the *Waesland*, bound for Philadelphia. A few hours out of port, the *Waesland* encountered heavy fog and collided with another ship. Although its crew and passengers were rescued, the steamer sank, dragging the Automat to the bottom of the sea. Fortunately, the machine was insured. In 1902, a second arrived in Philadelphia, just in time for the June 9 opening of the newest restaurant, at 818 Chestnut Street: the first Horn & Hardart Automat.

These early machines that came from Germany—there eventually would be four—were a far cry from the wall of streamlined rectangular glass doors that serve modern memory. The original ornate brass contrivances were crude, providing more novelty than speed. The food inside the little windows was actually a display, a sample of what one *could* order—not revealing the order itself. For hot dishes, customers bought a token from a cashier and deposited it into the coin slot for the desired food. They would then wait while a cook in the basement prepared their dish and cranked it up to the dining room on a dumbwaiter. A second token was inserted before the machine surrendered the dish. Obtaining cold food and desserts was a simpler matter, since they were already prepared. Still, the customer had to wait for the journey from basement to dining room. Coffee- and milk-dispensing machines were installed, although the now-familiar dolphin-head spout would not be introduced until Joe Horn came across the inspiration for them on a trip to Italy. (Two beverages to be found in the early Automats that did not survive into the mid-century were beer and wine.)

Three years later, in 1905, a second Automat opened at 101 South Juniper Street, followed by a third in 1907 at 909 Market Street. The last Automat imported from Germany was modified before a fourth Automat opened in 1912 at 21 South Eleventh Street. By now, Horn and Hardart had their chief engineer, John Fritsche, design a machine that would cater to American tastes. (Fritsche continued designing machines for Horn & Hardart until his death in 1947 at seventy-five.) He came up with the idea of a unit fronted by Carrara or milk glass on which hung four rectangular glass doors that would be operated by a knob. No tokens, no waiting for someone to put together your meal. All you had to do was make your selection, deposit a nickel, turn the knob, and the door sprang open and your sandwich or piece of pie awaited you.

What took place on the other side of the glass doors was

more complicated. In these new "automatic" restaurants, it took efficient manpower to keep the slots filled with food. At the back of each vertical column of windows was a metal drum that revolved on a pivot. Food was loaded onto the shelves of the drum from the back, then the drum was swung around so that the food faced the windows. Ice cream was kept cold by a motor-driven refrigerating plant and was served in the same way but with different drums. Hot machines had hot-water jackets that could keep dishes hot, such as deviled crabs and fish croquettes—two popular dishes in the early years. The only fully automatic machines served beverages: coffee, tea, milk, and chocolate milk poured out in measured amounts, operated by an electric pump.

To supply the nickels for the machines, Horn & Hardart installed glass-paned booths behind which sat the nickel throwers. "By the end of the day, your hands were absolutely filthy from the nickels," says former thrower Anne Downey. "You had to knock them off at five at a time. They would put money down and you would just flip off five nickels at a time for a quarter." The nickel throwers became a fascination.

With their great success in Philadelphia, the partners decided it was time to take this Automat to New York City. If the idea of a waiterless restaurant could take hold in the more leisurely paced Philadelphia, wouldn't it be perfect in the city where no one ever had enough time? In September 1910, Pennsylvania Station opened the doors to its monumental gateway on Seventh Avenue, just south of Thirty-fourth Street, giving the nation a second railroad entry into Manhattan (along with the newly modernized Grand Central Terminal). Every morning, ferryboats crossing the East and Hudson Rivers deposited commuters onto the city's congested sidewalks. The city's first subway line ran up the spine of Manhattan from City Hall to 145th Street. For a taste of Gotham's magic, tourists, commuters, and city dwellers all followed the trail of incandescent lights up Broadway to the Great White Way that was Times Square and the emerging theater district.

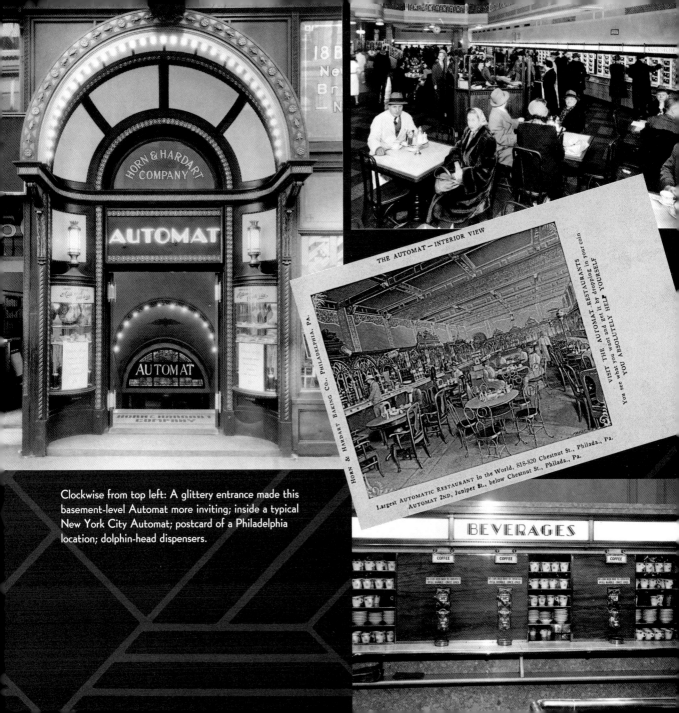

Clockwise from top left: A glittery entrance made this basement-level Automat more inviting; inside a typical New York City Automat; postcard of a Philadelphia location; dolphin-head dispensers.

I remember that big stained-glass window. I once met Rudy Vallee there. The management was very, very kind. They wouldn't tell people to go away when they were very busy. They would engage the customers in conversation until a table was available.

JOE FRANKLIN

Nicola D'Ascenzo's stained glass, Philadelphia.

In 1911, in anticipation of their entry into Manhattan, the partners formed the Horn & Hardart Co. of New York. By 1912, the same year the last of the German-made Automats was installed in Philadelphia, the newly patented American-made Automat was ready. The company decided to test the New York City market with two lunchrooms, neither of which was automatic. These small establishments were open only for lunch, serving coffee and baked items. To introduce their newly streamlined Automat, the company needed a sizable piece of property in a location that would draw hundreds of New Yorkers. They found it on Forty-sixth Street and Broadway, in the heart of Times Square, the crossroads of the bustling city. This would be their showcase, and they decided to spare no expense.

The first New York Automat was a literal jewel. Glass sculptor Nicola D'Ascenzo, who had designed the windows for the city's Cathedral of St. John the Divine and Washington, D.C.'s Folger Shakespeare Library, was commissioned to create a stained-glass window thirty feet wide and two stories high, rising just above the side-walk, its panels coming alive in the rays of Manhattan light. At its center, the word AUTOMAT was framed by garlands of fruit and flowers.

Inside, customers sat on walnut-stained chairs, at round, Carrara-glass-topped tables that held the Automat's condiment-laden signature lazy Susans. They would dine under another of D'Ascenzo's creations: a ceiling of richly colored carvings—tree boughs laden with fruit and foliage—radiating from a central column. The four beams that formed part of the column were lined with incandescent lightbulbs, giving off the feeling of dining under a splendid carousel. A white marble floor inlaid with large black circles added to the sense of pleasant motion, as did the wood-framed mirrors on the walls. Ceiling fans with thick wooden blades cooled customers in the sultry summer months.

There was no steam table, no cafeteria, just walls of that unique invention that some anonymous salesman had persuaded Frank Hardart to buy and that John Fritsche had streamlined for American tastes. In *Orange Roofs, Golden Arches,* Philip

Langdon describes those walls of vending machines as "not just machinery but machinery with splendor, its ornate wooden framework sparkling with beveled mirrored surfaces, its uppermost edges alternating between swelling arches and horizontals, so that the entire room was enveloped in an ennobling, continuous rhythm."

On July 2, the doors to Manhattan's first Automat opened, and New Yorkers began filing through. On that opening day, 8,693 nickels were slipped into the slots. Frank Hardart's famous French-drip coffee poured from the mouths of dolphins, the sea creatures that had enchanted Joe Horn when he came upon them on a fountain in Pistoia del Greci, near Florence, Italy.

But what most delighted the jaded citizens of Gotham was the ability to get an excellent-tasting, nourishing meal and a great cup of coffee for nickels, all in a beautiful setting that gave them the autonomy they prized while somehow making them feel at home. This was more than a successful restaurant. It was the beginning of a beautiful empire.

Clockwise from top left: The Empire State Building; an early Automat in New York City; Nicola D'Ascenzo's stained glass façade at the Times Square Automat; Tony Curtis in *The Rat Race*, 1960.

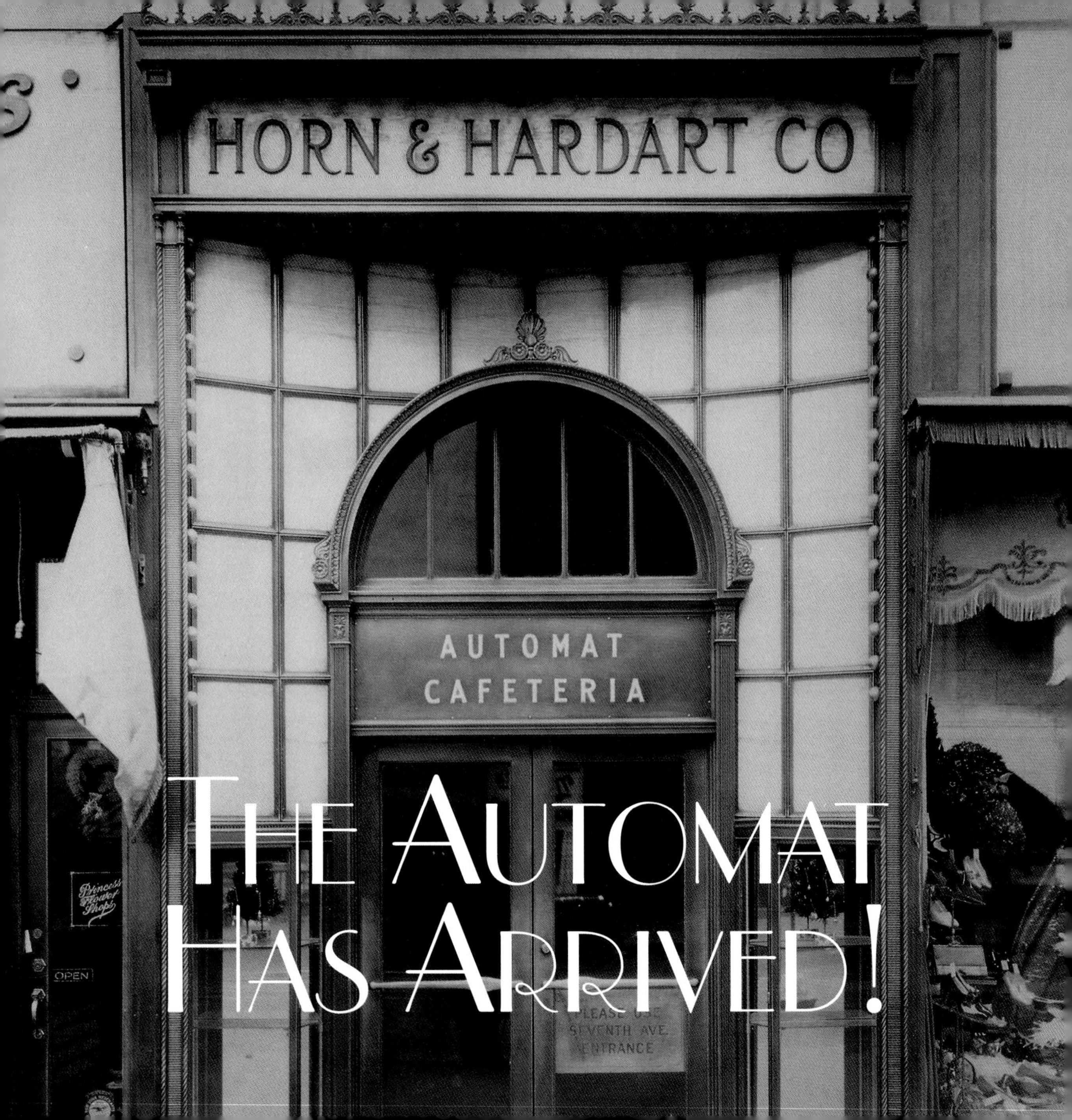

The Automat Has Arrived!

Oh, man. I lived in the Automat. They had the greatest chocolate milk.

When I moved to Philadelphia, I apportioned less than two dollars

a day to eat on, and the Automat was the only place I could do it.

DICK CLARK

It didn't take long for Horn & Hardart Automats, cafeterias, and restaurants to begin sprouting up all over New York and Philadelphia. At the turn of the century, the American city—particularly New York—was beginning to see its future, and that future was faster-paced. In the decade between 1900 and 1910, the city's population rose by 50 percent. Women were entering the workforce, taking jobs as stenographers, typists, and secretaries or working behind the counters of Macy's and Gimbel's, the new rivals on Herald Square. A whole new labor force of women was occupying America's cities, all of whom needed a place to have a quick, inexpensive, and nourishing

Opposite: An ornate New York City entrance. Above: A delivery truck.

lunch in an atmosphere that wasn't intimidating. The trick was to offer eating places that combined speed and efficiency with a certain amount of gentility.

Cafeterias became the testing ground for this new lifestyle. In New York City, the one chain that understood precisely how to handle this transition was Childs. By 1900, Childs had nine cafeterias in Manhattan, all sparkling-white emporiums where waitresses in starched uniforms could pass for nurses. Offsetting the reassuring antiseptic cleanliness were crystal chandeliers, offering a suitable nod to the delicate sensibilities of the women they hoped to attract. Six years later, Schrafft's appeared, catering to working women, emphasizing home cooking in proper dining rooms. Bickfords cafeterias followed, much like Horn & Hardarts, with one big exception: They had no walls of vending machines.

It was the vending machines that propelled Horn & Hardart into the minds and hearts of New Yorkers. In a 1986 interview, Gus Hardart, vice-president and secretary, said, "At the time, people were fascinated by mechanical things. The automobile was just breaking on to the scene, and here was a mechanical device for making food. It caught everyone's imagination."

They also appealed to a city that had claimed its independence, not only from the rigidity of the Victorian past, but from the more structured lifestyles of the rest of the country. New Yorkers of every strata loved their autonomy over the little glass door. There was no waiting and no ordering ritual as a censoring waiter mentally counted his tip. There were no tips. There was just you and whatever took your fancy.

"Customers could choose not only what sort of food they desired, but the actual piece from among several on offer. The New York outlet featured these machines in abundance, presenting a glass-cased cornucopia to the crowds of Times Square," wrote Alec Tristin Shuldiner in his dissertation *Trapped Behind the Automat: Technological Systems and the American Restaurant, 1902–1991*. You could order three desserts and forget the sandwich. The vending machines had so captured the imaginations of New Yorkers that people often referred to Horn & Hardart simply as the Automat.

In the 1910s, New York City had fifteen Horn & Hardart Automats. In September 1922, its first combination Automat-cafeteria was introduced, heralded in newspaper ads as the largest restaurant in New York City, with a capacity to feed ten thousand customers per day. Still catering to turn-of-the-century epicurean sensibilities, the Automat-cafeterias offered a more eccentric fare than the nurture food for which the chain later became popular. Items like milk toast, oyster stew, Berliner rolls, fried ham with wine jelly, and something called cabinet pudding (probably a loose, milk-based dish) were standard items. In addition to the usual condiments, the lazy Susans held Lea & Perrins Worcestershire sauce and shakers full of celery salt. If a customer asked for tea, the "coffeeman" would cut a piece of cheesecloth into a small square, fill it with one-sixteenth of an ounce of loose tea, fold it, and tie it with a string; it was then placed in an individual teapot and served. During the years when World War I was raging, only one teaspoon of sugar was allowed per customer. There were also wheatless, meatless, and heatless days, which all restaurants had to endure.

Stand-up round tables topped with Carrara glass were a feature in all New York Horn & Hardarts, probably a holdover from the oyster parlors that were popular into the nineteenth century. According to Carl Uehlinger Sr., one of Horn & Hardart's old-timers, the Automat at 1241 Broadway had a soda fountain at its front entrance and linen napkins on every table. Customers could also purchase cigars and cigarettes.

By 1932, there were forty-two Automat-cafeterias in New York City. Philadelphia had forty-six restaurants, fewer than half of which had Automats. Many of the Philadelphia Horn & Hardarts were combinations of cafeterias and service restaurants.

In 1922, Horn & Hardart introduced its retail stores, a revolutionary idea for the time, where prepackaged Automat meals and desserts were sold over the counter. In

Left: An early interior.

the twenties, few wives were in the workforce, and the only contact they had with Horn & Hardart's food were the praises from their husbands' mouths (or perhaps a taste of the unfinished lunches they brought home). On November 22, just before Thanksgiving, the company decided to open a temporary retail shop in their vacant store at 1425 Chestnut Street. It was so successful that they reopened it for the Christmas crowds. Shortly thereafter, permanent fixtures were installed and the store officially opened as the first Horn & Hardart retail shop. Joe Horn hired Ike Clements of the Clements Advertising Agency, who initiated an ad campaign using the now-famous slogan, "Less Work for Mother." The idea was to seduce housewives into buying these precooked meals with the promise that they would free up time for leisure. It also gave them a taste of the food they had been missing. Eventually, eighty-four retail shops, many located near elevated and subway stops, would appear in both cities.

In the beginning, the popular restaurants with their attached retail shops were an architectural hodgepodge. Some, like the Horn & Hardart on Manhattan's Broadway and Thirty-seventh Street and the very opulent one in Philadelphia's equally opulent Earle Theatre Building on Eleventh and Market Streets, were in leased spaces, tucked away in basements. Then there was the Horn & Hardart at 68 Trinity Place in lower Manhattan—New York City's flagship Automat—just in back of the Trinity churchyard. Horn & Hardart would occupy three floors (ground floor, basement, and subbasement) of the new six-story, company-owned building designed by Frederick Putnam Platt. Eventually, this Horn & Hardart would have its own commissary, which would serve all Horn & Hardarts below Fourteenth Street.

Even the restaurant interiors, though quite opulent, were not that consistent. The Earle Theatre Building's restaurant boasted bottoncino marble walls and stairways, and glass lighting fixtures decorated with tiny figures of fish and fowl. The 232 Market Street location had Corinthian columns and Renaissance-style candelabra. Aside from John Fritsche's familiar white Carrara glass walls of vending machines and Nicola D'Ascenzo's trademark stained-glass windows, which had been installed in many of the Philadelphia restaurants, there was little architectural consistency among the growing number of Automats and cafeterias. But that was about to change.

On December 17, 1929, just days before the company's thirty-eighth birthday, a new Horn & Hardart opened in Philadelphia on the corner of Sixteenth and Chestnut Streets, on the site of a razed 1871 historic mansion. Part of an eight-story building that would serve as the company's headquarters, this was another showpiece, touted as "Philadelphia's Most Beautiful Restaurant." This Horn & Hardart boasted Italian marble walls and a grand stairway leading to the great window that had been designed by D'Ascenzo; hand-painted zodiac signs arched above its stone entranceway. And in addition to the Automat and cafeteria, a full-service restaurant was installed on the first floor and mezzanine. But what made this latest addition to the Horn & Hardart chain special was the architect who designed it.

Ralph B. Bencker was considered the preeminent Art Deco architect of Philadelphia. His work on the apartment complex on Rittenhouse Square introduced the new *moderne* "vertical style" of architecture to the City of Brotherly Love, a style that Bencker felt captured the spirit of America as it emerged into the twentieth century. Bencker wasn't alone in finding expression for his time in a style that was somewhat theatrical. "We were very influenced by movies," says architectural historian Justin Ferate. "Think of Ginger Rogers and Fred Astaire dancing down those polished stairs. Architecture became a stage set." Ferate also sees the Art Deco style serving as a grand escape from the memory of World War I. "We wanted to push the war far behind us. Art Deco design was very romantic, very glamorous."

For the facade of the new Horn & Hardart, Bencker chose a pale blush-colored stone, molding it into the soft Deco lines that would become the trademark for thirty-nine more Horn & Hardart restaurants and retail shops in New York City and Philadelphia. That design would culminate in the Horn & Hardart on Fifty-seventh Street between Sixth and Seventh Avenues in Manhattan. "Perhaps the finest Art Deco restaurant exterior," Philip Langdon wrote of Ralph Bencker's 1938 masterpiece. "It exuded an exuberant modern spirit in curving pink terra-cotta."

That spirit, fostered by optimism from a still-soaring stock market, expressed itself dramatically in the architecture of cities. In New York, skyscrapers climbed to the clouds. Some, like the Chanin Building, turned lobbies into museums of fanciful flora and fauna. The new modernism, with sleek, geometric lines and subtext of motion, had been propelled by the machine age, particularly by Henry Ford, who gave the country wheels. What could be

Below: Art Deco's crowning achievement, the Chrysler Building in New York City. Opposite: Automats once featured shellfish dishes.

more liberating than Model Ts dropping off those endless assembly lines, ready to be driven anywhere?

The marriage of the machine age and architecture reached its pinnacle in Manhattan the same year that Ralph B. Bencker designed Horn & Hardart's Sixteenth and Chestnut Streets restaurant, with the completion of the Chrysler Building. Architect William Van Alen's Art Deco masterpiece was a poem to the automobile. Beneath its gleaming spire and spoked upper windows, shiny gargoyles and symbolic friezes evoked automobile ornaments and hubcaps. It was also so theatrical that Van Alen appeared at the Beaux Arts Ball dressed as his building.

Two years later, the eighty-five-story Empire State Building rose even higher, topped with a 200-foot signal tower intended to serve as a mooring mast for dirigibles. That idea was never realized, but imagine the dramatic entrance one would have made into the heart of the city, descending from an open gangway a thou-

OWICHES   SANDWICHES   SANDW

I liked it because it was free and open. It was well lit and you could see all you were

going to eat in those little cubicles. For a kid, that was fun. I liked the cherry pie.

TONY CURTIS

sand feet in the air. Through the dark days of the Depression, Rockefeller Center and Radio City Music Hall were built, giving the city its quintessential Art Deco stage set.

By 1935, a Pennsylvanian visiting a Horn & Hardart in New York City could ride the Pennsylvania Railroad's *Broadway Limited* powered by industrial designer Raymond Loewy's sleek GG-1 locomotives. These streamlined, rivet-free engines, like the New York Central's aptly named *Twentieth Century,* exemplified the blending of function with romance, giving the public one more object with which to fall in love. Interestingly, Loewy was later commissioned to design the facades of Cushman's, a New York bakery chain. Like Bencker, Loewy chose a light surface (white porcelain-enameled metal panels were used on the facade) and curved, nautical lines for the windows. Today, Bencker's Art Deco gem on Fifty-seventh Street, which has withstood numerous incarnations, is occupied by Shelly's restaurant.

As their popularity soared, Horn & Hardarts in every combination kept popping up. Bencker's hand was seen in the basement restaurant at Broad and Chestnut Streets, and the street-level one at Juniper and Market Streets. Healthy profits convinced the company to purchase the building it leased in the Germantown section. By 1930, Philadelphia had forty-six Horn & Hardart restaurants, just under half of which had Automats.

In Manhattan, huge newspaper ads would sometimes accompany the opening of a new Automat. "Across from the Roxy Theater" was the caption for a sketch in a 1927 ad for a new Horn & Hardart. Seventh Avenue and Fiftieth Street got a large new Horn & Hardart, as did Fifth Avenue and Forty-fifth Street. Eighth Avenue and the major crosstown streets had several. By 1930, one was installed on upper Broadway at 110th Street, and in September 1932, the Bronx got its first Automat, a modern Bencker building on 170th Street. Brooklyn followed in June of 1936 on Willoughby Street in the Borough Hall section, this one a Bencker modernistic structure in terra-cotta and bronze. And on August 11, 1934, another architectural gem rose on West 181st Street,

a celebration of Art Deco featuring a huge skylight of art glass depicting Manhattan Island, with replicas of the Empire State and Chrysler Buildings etched into its surface. A beautifully detailed mezzanine wound its way above the dining room.

There was no question that Horn & Hardart and the Automat were fast becoming part of the lexicon of Philadelphians and New Yorkers. But what elevated the Automat from a novel convenience to a culinary institution that survived into the 1960s was not just Frank Hardart's secret-recipe coffee or John Fritsche's genius in redesigning the German vending machines to American tastes, providing the Automat with its signature novelty. It was Joseph Horn's insatiable appetite for good food and the idea he had come up with—back when the partners had only a handful of lunchrooms—to deliver it.

Left: An elaborate Art Deco interior, New York City. Right: The interior of the West 181st Street Automat, New York City.

Baked Macaroni and Cheese

serves 4 to 6

¼ pound rigatoni macaroni

2 tablespoons unsalted butter, plus more for greasing pan

1½ tablespoons all-purpose flour

¼ teaspoon salt

¼ teaspoon freshly ground white pepper

1½ cups milk

½ pound sharp Cheddar cheese, cut into ¼-inch cubes

½ teaspoon Worcestershire sauce

Cook the macaroni according to package directions. Drain.

Preheat the oven to 375°F.

In a 1-quart saucepan, melt the butter over low heat. With a wire whisk, mix in the flour, salt, and pepper. Cook 1 to 2 minutes, or until a smooth mixture forms. Continue to whisk and gradually add the milk; cook about 5 minutes, until the mixture is thick and smooth. Remove from heat.

In a large mixing bowl, combine the cooked macaroni with the sauce, cheese, and Worcestershire sauce. Pour into a buttered 8 × 8 × 2 pan and bake for 25 minutes, or until the top browns.

Chocolate-Chip Cookies

makes about 30

¾ cup vegetable shortening

½ cup granulated sugar

½ cup brown sugar

1 teaspoon baking soda

¼ teaspoon salt

½ teaspoon vanilla extract

1 large egg

1½ cups all-purpose flour

9-ounce bag semi-sweet chocolate chips

Preheat the oven to 375°F.

In an electric mixer, blend the shortening with the white and brown sugars until light and fluffy, about 5 minutes. Add the baking soda, salt, vanilla, and eggs, and beat until mixed. Stir in the flour slowly and beat at low speed until well blended. Fold in the chocolate chips.

Drop the mixture by rounded tablespoonfuls, 2 inches apart, onto an ungreased cookie sheet. Bake 10 to 12 minutes, until lightly browned. With a metal spatula, remove the cookies to wire racks to cool. Repeat with the remaining dough. Store the cookies in a tightly covered container.

THOSE BAKED BEANS!
AND THAT COCONUT PIE!

The first time I came to New York, I had a meal at the Automat. I had heard about the Automat, and I had to go to see what it was all about.

LEONARD NIMOY

How did they do it? A customer could drop into any one of the Horn & Hardart Automats and cafeterias in New York and Philadelphia, at any time of the day, put a couple of nickels into one of the vending-machine slots, and pull out a piece of pie, a crock of baked beans, or a macaroni-and-cheese casserole that tasted exactly as it had the day before.

Opposite: A retail shop in New York City, right next to the subway. Above: A hearty cup of soup.

From the beginning, Philadelphia had its commissary, a narrow four-story building at Tenth and Warnock Streets that by 1926 had been expanded three times. In 1912, the same year New York City got its first Automat, Frank and his son Augustin Hardart purchased a piece of land from the Astor estate, on Fiftieth Street and Eleventh Avenue. (The Astor estate refused to deal with any corporate interests, so the cousins as individuals bought it, then turned it over to the company.) Two years later, a six-story building was on the site, the company's New York commissary, serving the fifteen Automats. By 1921, seventeen Automats were dotting the streets of New York, and several of them had cafeterias. Before the commissary went into gear, rolls were purchased from Howard's Bakery, and sausages were made for the Automat by Henry Hauck, a butcher on Ninth Avenue. Once the commissary was up and running, mass production was raised to an art.

Each day at five in the morning, a fleet of Edison trucks was dispatched to the docks and the city's markets to pick up the ingredients that went into 2,500 rolls and loaves of bread, 3,000 pies and 44,000 individual cakes, 300 gallons of soup, 200 gallons of baked beans, and 1,200 pounds of ham. Horn & Hardart bought the highest quality meat and produce, usually purchasing huge quantities when prices were low. If the quality of an ingredient that went into one of their dishes wasn't up to snuff, the dish would be temporarily removed from their menus. At the commissary, a small army of employees manned revolving knives, band saws, and mechanical agitators to peel apples, cut meat, and mix mayo, while huge steam kettles cooked up the soup.

Bread began as mounds of dough that were placed in long, traveling ovens, emerging at the other end as golden-brown loaves. Other ovens resembling Ferris wheels took in dough at one spot, then turned full circle before giving off baked buns. The famous huckleberry, pumpkin, and custard pies required a quartet of employees working in perfect synchronization at a revolving table. The first man placed a pie plate on a frame and covered it with a sheet of dough. The second man added the filling. A third man placed a top crust over it. And the fourth man trimmed the edges and marked the dough to indicate the type of filling. Six pies a minute were processed and slipped onto one of the Ferris-wheel ovens for baking. Rosemary Hardart-Wylie, daughter of Tom Hardart, a former president, remembers taking a tour with her family when her father was president: "The commissary was filled with conveyer belts that wrapped around rooms several times and took food through the ovens, and then around to cool, and then into the next room where they were boxed. I remember the huge vats of cookies, too, and a big mixing bowl for bread."

Cooked foods were kept fresh-tasting by refrigerating them immediately. Seymour Schneider, director of special inspection services for the Department of Health, remembers a tubelike machine encased in a refrigerant with a spiral device inside that carried the food along. "They would pump the creamed spinach from a vat into this machine. That refrigerant made it cold immediately, and then they packed it and sent it out to the stores."

To make sure the baked beans tasted the same as they did the day before and the day before that, Joe Horn came up with a unique idea: Have the quality of his food judged by company executives, managers from various restaurants, the commissary's head chef, and in Philadelphia Joe Horn himself, known for his enormous appetite. Each afternoon at precisely 12:30, the group would gather in a spartan room set aside in both the New York and Philadelphia commissaries. In New York City, Frank Hardart presided, and after his death, a line of Hardarts, including Frank Hardart Jr., Augustin Hardart, Tom Hardart (Frank Jr.'s son), and Augustin Hardart Jr. "On the personal level, quality control extended to the home front," says Nancy Hardart, widow of Augustin Hardart Jr. "Frozen food was discouraged. And there was no fooling him. He always knew."

Both rooms had a long wooden table, officially known as the Sample Table. In front of each hardback chair was a small pile of knives, forks, and spoons and a coffee cup kept filled for palate-cleansing between each dish. A large blackboard hung on one wall, listing items of food. On a given day, it wasn't unusual to see three kinds

of soup, a main dish, several desserts—including duplicates of one pie—and if the company was thinking of making a switch, two kinds of butter. It was no wonder that some executives who had to endure these daily tastings referred to it as the "Ulcer Table." Although the Sample Tables in both cities had the same kind of foods, there were exceptions: New Yorkers liked their stewed tomatoes slightly sweeter and their cheeses stronger. They would not go near scrapple (fried ground pork and cornmeal), a favorite in Philadelphia. To Joe Horn, the daily tasting was the keystone of Horn & Hardart's success, and he insisted that every company executive in both cities be present.

Executives weren't the only individuals whose opinions counted: In every Horn & Hardart Automat and cafeteria, customer complaints were taken seriously. At the end of each day, managers from each of the restaurants would relay any negative remarks about the food to the commissaries. Those comments were brought up the following day at the Sample Table. Bill Curtis, a former president who started with the company as a night cashier, remembered the process as being very democratic: "Customers from the stores and restaurants as well as employees could write comments. Any level of employee could be critical. There were no repercussions for negative feedback. You said what was on your mind." The company's reputation was less about selling itself than it was about delivering. "We had a slogan—'The Public Appreciates Quality,'" said Curtis. "We were careful to live up to this. Food was healthy. If something wasn't right, it was taken off the list rather than disguised."

Horn & Hardart's emphasis on freshness extended, in a very unique way, to how they ordered their eggs. Unlike many restaurants that relied on frozen eggs, Horn & Hardart ordered their eggs fresh from the

Above: Employees behind the steam table. Right: Making a
selection; note the lazy Susan for condiments.

Manhattan Egg Company. Not only were they fresh, they were "broken out." "There was an egg-breaking establishment on Greenwich Street in lower Manhattan that had probably one hundred women, and all they did was break open eggs," says Seymour Schneider. "They had girls just sitting there with a long tube that was almost like a vacuum cleaner. It would suck up any odors so that they could determine if there were any bad eggs." The eggs were broken at room temperature to maximize the amount of egg white extracted, then placed in thirty-pound cans, which went into refrigerated hundred-pound stainless-steel tubs for delivery to the commissary.

In the early Philadelphia years, both Joe Horn and Frank Hardart were present at the daily tastings; when Frank died in 1918, Joe kept up the habit. He was even known to show up at restaurants unannounced, tasting food behind the steam counter. Soup was always kept covered to keep it from becoming too salty. "The steam, which is really the condensate of that soup, is gradually leaving the soup," says Seymour Schneider. "What doesn't leave is the salt. The Automat always covered their soup."

Horn also made sure the people behind the counter adhered to the standards set in the two-hundred-plus-page, leather-bound company bible that he created and dispensed to every manager, known as the Manager's Rule Book. Instructions were detailed on how to order ingredients from the commissary and how to cook items for the cafeteria that had not been prepared ahead of time. A 1941 rule book has recipes for fish dishes that appear to be aimed at a surprisingly sophisticated palate: Creamed finnan haddie and lobster à la king were on the menu as well as panned oysters. Seven plump oysters sautéed in top-quality butter could be had for forty-five cents. A veal chop with two vegetables cost thirty-five cents. And Horn & Hardart's famous coffee required two gallons of water to one pound of coffee, with elaborate instructions on how to clean all utensils and prepare the coffee. The finished product had to undergo a taste test before being sold to customers. Sometimes the taster was Joe Horn, who would slip into an Automat unannounced, sip the coffee, and if it wasn't up to standard, send it back and insist that a fresh batch be brewed. Even without Horn's presence, coffee was never allowed to stand for more than an hour. Both the coffee and the freshly squeezed orange juice were tossed after two hours. A manager who was caught not following this rule was given a stern warning.

Long after Horn's death, his rules were enforced. "My dad was a stickler and noticed whenever the book wasn't followed," says Madeline Hardart of her father, Tom Hardart, then president. "It included things like cutting English muffins with a fork instead of a knife."

Another of Joe Horn's unbendable rules was that no unsold food be held over for another day. Anything that was left would be taken to Horn & Hardart's day-old shops. Horn's commitment to consistency and quality reached every Automat and cafeteria in both cities. His presence was so strong that even after his death in 1941, the best compliment an executive at the Sample Table could give a dish was to say, "Mr. Horn would have liked this."

A child's delight—choosing one's own meal at the Reading Terminal Automat, Philadelphia.

It was this obsessive attention to quality that won the hearts of New Yorkers and Philadelphians. Just as people react to great architecture, Horn & Hardart customers were quick to grasp that this pride was directed at them; the two-city chain cared enough about the people it served to make sure they were never disappointed. With the ritual of the Sample Table, Horn & Hardart was saying that the palates of its customers—including those with just a handful of change—were the barometer by which the company conducted its business. As a result, the Automat became one of the few constants in lives that would soon take some dramatic and unexpected turns.

Everybody's Going to the Automat

Said the Technocrat, to the Plutocrat

To the Autocrat, and the Democrat —

"Let's all go eat at the Automat!"

"OUR ECONOMIC SITUATION IN AN EGGSHELL,"
New York Evening Sun, February 23, 1933

On June 21, 1930, actress Jean Harlow made the *New York World-Telegram* when she bolted from her publicity tour for her film *Hell's Angels* to satisfy a major ambition: get herself to an Automat, plunk four nickels into a vending slot, and taste those famous baked beans. She wasn't alone. The Countess de Guell, lady-in-waiting to the Queen of Spain, tried her hand at the slots. Shaha Buddin Kahn, an Afghan chief, weary of his entourage of servants, reportedly liked to slip into the Automat and fetch his own food. Socialite Gloria Vanderbilt's comments made

Oppostie: A busy Philadelphia Automat. Above: A 1926 cartoon of a formal dinner at the White House.

A 1931 newspaper ad illustrates
Horn & Hardart's role in the
Depression.

another newspaper. "Next to El Morocco, I like the Automat best. I like to poke nickels into the little slots and be free to move around among people unrecognized." And actor Gene Kelly, who was appearing on Broadway in Rodgers and Hart's *Pal Joey,* was caught by *Look* magazine in front of one of the Automat's dolphin-head juice dispensers, sharing breakfast with his wife, actress Betsy Blair.

Joseph Horn and Frank Hardart really got it right. Give the working guy and gal an inexpensive quality meal in an attractive, familiar setting, keep the place shipshape, and dispense with the need to tip, and you've got yourself a great success. What the partners didn't anticipate was the stream of celebrities who came through their doors. "New York in those days had only two types: Park Avenue and the workers. But they all came to the Automat," wrote senior executive vice-president Robert F. Byrnes in a 1982 *New York Times* op-ed piece.

In the 1930s and 1940s, hardly a day passed when there wasn't some mention in one of the newspapers about some happening at the Automat. When an abandoned toddler was found in the Fourteenth Street Automat on Christmas Eve, newspapers dubbed him "The Automat Baby." Columnists loved stories on the Automat. Danton Walker's "Broadway," Leonard Lyons's "The Lyons' Den," and Dorothy Kilgallen's "Voice of Broadway" were just three of the columns that regularly included items. Walter Winchell wrote in his uniquely coined jargon of "hungry school kids every *Satdee* noon rushing in for their *Automatinees.*" When Otto Van Hapsburg, pretender to the Austro-Hungarian throne, slipped into the Fifty-seventh Street Automat, New Yorkers learned that he dined on pot roast, baked beans, and beets. Sister Elizabeth Kenny—dubbed "The Angel" for her work with polio victims—made the *New York Mirror* in 1949 when she turned down a luncheon at a swank restaurant, bringing her group to the same Automat where Van Hapsburg enjoyed his pot roast.

Celebrities from screen siren Veronica Lake to evangelist Aimee Semple McPherson made the newspapers when they showed up at the Automat, as did John D. Rockefeller Jr. when he chose it for a dinner break from a conference of the Interchurch World Movement. At one point, a column called "Automat Notes" appeared in several newspapers, offering food-related tidbits. Another food column in newspapers, "What's Your Favorite?," invited famous personalities to share their favorite recipes and once featured actor Gregory Peck scrambling his eggs "Oscar" as he praised Horn & Hardart's version. "I have always thought that the Automat in New York has the best scrambled eggs in the world," said Peck.

But it was the Depression that brought the Automat into the culinary mainstream. As people lost their jobs and breadlines formed, a clever Horn & Hardart newspaper ad showed how the company tapped into the need to economize without sacrificing dignity (see sidebar, right).

Encouraging down-on-their-luck New Yorkers to visit their Automats was a good idea, but Horn & Hardart didn't stop there. Another ad appearing in the March 16, 1931, *New York Evening Journal* pledged a day's receipts from the Horn & Hardart Automat-cafeteria at Fifth Avenue and Forty-fifth Street, and the one at 68 Trinity Place—its two largest restaurants—to the Relief of the Emergency Employment Committee & Women's Fund Committee of New York. "Help the Man Who Wants to Work," the ad proclaimed. The message was clear: We're all in this together, and Horn & Hardart was willing to do its share. A year later, the company trimmed an hour from all of its day and night shifts, providing extra work for two hundred employees without shaving wages.

"*You know you're just as welcome when you spend a Nickel as when you spend a Dollar (and you can get a hearty, satisfying meal without even beginning to pay as much as that). That's why the Horn & Hardart Automat-Cafeterias are increasingly popular in this Era of Thrift.*"

(UNITED PRESS PHOTO)

Celebrities

Take

Coffee Break

at Automat

Yes, your Automats make news. Maybe you have never had the pleasure of meeting a real live celebrity face to face, but like all the rest of us, people in the news like good food, fast service and pleasant surroundings. The couple above is typical.

Crooner Eddie Fisher and his lovely wife, actress Debbie Reynolds, share a hasty tete-a-tete at the Automat across from Penn Station at 461 Eighth Avenue. Afterwards, the pair hurried to catch a train. Later that day, Debbie's mother announced in Hollywood that the young star was expecting a child next November.

So be on the lookout in serving your customer. Bet it won't be long before you meet somebody whose name and picture are well known to everybody.

Clockwise from top left: Debbie Reynolds and Eddie Fisher catching a snack at the Automat near Penn Station, New York City; at 250 West Forty-second Street, New York City; an Automat book of cartoons and jokes, 1929.

All of this beneficence paid off. In 1932, when sixty thousand New Yorkers were evicted from their apartments in the first three frigid months, Horn & Hardart's forty-three Automat-cafeterias and twenty-two retail shops cleared a profit of more than $1.5 million. In Philadelphia, ten thousand people were employed in the forty-six restaurants and twenty-eight retail shops whose profits totaled a million dollars. In the two years following the 1929 stock-market crash, the Automat's volume of sales increased by 50 percent. The only loss of money occurred when people put slugs in the slots instead of nickels. In 1936, Horn & Hardart printed a guidebook of Philadelphia. Among the historic sites that the booklet described was a section on the company's Automats, cafeterias, and retail shops. What was particularly astounding was that the chain that started out by specializing in comfort food for the working class had not only put itself on the nation's map, it had managed to invite the rich and famous to share a table with the guy who didn't have a job.

The Automats themselves had become more inviting. In keeping with the more modern, less formal times, large plate-glass windows replaced the ornate Nicola D'Ascenzo stained glass, giving those on the outside a clear idea of what was going on inside. Automat signs, once lit by a string of 25-watt bulbs, were now illuminated with neon. Banished were window displays with fussy vases and fruit arrangements that were meant to put the turn-of-the-century female customer at ease. By now, everyone walking through one of Horn & Hardart's revolving doors knew exactly what to expect. That was part of its comfort appeal.

More than just a place to catch an inexpensive meal or to nurse that nickel cup of coffee when a nickel was all you had, the Automat served as a hearth for the soul, a place where all New Yorkers and Philadelphians could go to keep the cold reality of hard times at bay. Even though customers were spending less, more people were eating their meals at Horn & Hardart, both in New York City and Philadelphia. "My mother was scraping the bottom of her purse, trying to find coins," said Deborah Harkins, a child of the 1940s whose post-Depression Philadelphia family had to deal with its own harsh economics.

"My father pooled all the coins and said to the family, 'All right, fifteen cent limit.' For fifteen cents, you could get baked beans, mashed potatoes, and creamed spinach. I can't remember a more harmonious moment in our family than when we all walked into that revolving door."

On New Year's Day in 1931, when the Depression was a very grim reality, "High Hat," a column appearing in a periodical called *Judge*, encouraged New Yorkers to celebrate New Year's Eve at the Automat:

> No money? Try Automat. "There will be plenty of actors to keep you company. What's wrong with the Automat for New Year's Eve? Lemons and cracked ice are free, incidentally. You'll find them at the iced tea slot."

In 1933, when many restaurants were trimming their staffs, Horn & Hardart hired chef Francis J. Bourdon to oversee the New York City commissary, giving him culinary control over all of the food that was served in the city's Automats. Bourdon, who remained with the firm for thirty-four years, wasn't just any chef. Trained at Le Cordon Bleu in Paris, he worked at hotels in Paris, Monte Carlo, Nice, Buenos Aires, and London. In New York City, he supervised the kitchens of the Plaza and Sherry-Netherland Hotels before coming to Horn & Hardart. It may be that in this fourth year of the Depression, when even the rich were eating out less, Bourdon was happy to work for a successful cafeteria chain, even though their carefully crafted, no-frills recipes left little room for his society-pleasing French touch. For Horn & Hardart, hiring this world-renowned chef—who never appeared without his crisp white toque—was as much about publicity as it was about maintaining the quality of the dishes coming from the commissary.

"The Horn & Hardart Automats were a great convenience for a young man in a hurry. They were also a blessing for all during the Depression. You could get as much or as little as you wanted, depending on your pocketbook."

RALPH EDWARDS,
Former Host,
The Horn & Hardart Children's Hour

Once a year, Bourdon was given free reign when he whipped up some special creations and entered them in a culinary contest sponsored by the Chefs de Cuisine Association of America. In one year, prize-winning platters of Sweetbreads Printanier, Parfait of Fatted Goose Liver Perigourdine, and an array of decorated cakes were placed on display in the window of Horn & Hardart's Times Square store. He outdid himself in 1939, with truffle-stuffed saddle of veal and a dessert tray that included a prize-winning wedding cake, all centered around a sugar-spun statue of Diana complete with a hound. This creation, along with the dishes, were placed in the window of the 1725 Broadway store.

None of these creations found themselves behind the glass slots of the vending machines or at the steam tables. And if they had been there, only the brave and the curious would have sampled them. In the 1930s and 1940s, the city did not yet have a large middle class. "Middle class—who ever heard of the middle class?" wrote Robert Byrnes. In his *New York Times* article, Byrnes described a typical family living in Brooklyn, the Bronx, or Queens taking the el to the big city, "dressed up, to the teeth" for their Thanksgiving dinner at the Times Square Automat. "Daddy and Mommy deposit the kids at the wooden tables with bentwood chairs. On top is a lazy Susan with all the condiments you could ever want in life. Daddy picks up a steaming dish: turkey and dressing (25 cents); two vegetables (10 cents), cranberries (5 cents). The kids loved the machines. They squeaked when they were hoisted to put a nickle [sic] two or three in the slot, turn the handle, pop up the window and get baked beans, baked macaroni and cheese, beef pie, chicken pies, the desserts." As Byrnes said, "It made you feel like a somebody and didn't cost an arm and a leg."

The Automat was first and foremost a working man's eating place. If movie stars and socialites dropped in, that was fine. But Joe Horn never lost sight of the fact that the "House That Nickels Built" owed its allegiance to the common folk who sustained it.

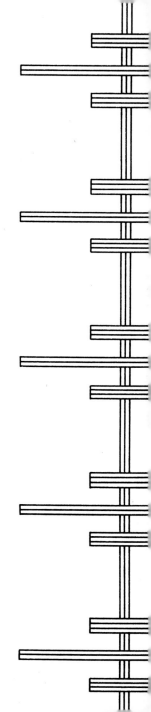

I'd finish work around four a.m. The Automat was the last place to go before you went home. I went in for a nice cup of hot chocolate for five cents. But what amazed me most of all were those cashiers. If you gave the lady a quarter, in one flick she'd throw five nickels at you. They were so accurate, it was amazing.

DOMINIC BUSCAGLIA, Former Bartender

Beef and Noodles with Burgundy Sauce

The original recipe called for Burgundy wine, which is rather expensive now—and was most likely not used at the time. Any hardy red wine will do.

serves 4 to 6

2 pounds lean beef (chuck or round) well trimmed and cut into ½-inch cubes

1 teaspoon salt

¼ teaspoon freshly ground black pepper

¼ cup all-purpose flour

2 tablespoons vegetable oil

1 medium carrot, grated

1 medium yellow onion, grated

1 celery rib, finely minced

2 garlic cloves, finely minced

1 bay leaf

2 cubes beef bouillon

½ cup tomato juice

1½ cups red wine

½ pound egg noodles

Season the beef with salt and pepper. Dredge in the flour and shake off the excess. Heat the oil in a large heavy-bottomed pan or Dutch oven over medium-high flame. Add the meat in batches, being careful not to crowd the pan, and sear on all sides until lightly browned, 3 to 5 minutes.

When all the pieces are browned, return all to the pan and add ½ cup water and all the other ingredients except the noodles. Bring to a boil, reduce the heat to low, cover, and simmer until tender, about 3½ to 4 hours.

When the beef is nearly done, cook the noodles according to package directions and drain. Just before serving, remove the bay leaf from the stew and mix in the freshly cooked noodles.

Opposite: Streetscape with elevated train, New York City, 1940s.

THE WAR YEARS

Funny people would sit at your table. They wore hair nets and too much makeup. In those days everyone could afford to live in New York.

BERNADETTE PETERS

February 25, 1945, was like New Year's Eve in New York City. Bands played into the wee hours and champagne corks popped. The only people who weren't celebrating were the club and restaurant owners. The next night, at the stroke of twelve, they would all become Cinderellas, turning in the tuxedos and dinner jackets for aprons and brooms.

Opposite: Automat interior, with bare shelves in the retail shop. Above: A 1938 *New Yorker* cover.

As part of the city's war effort, Mayor Fiorello La Guardia imposed an amusement curfew. Unlike the "dim-outs" three years before when Broadway's lights and those in buildings above the tenth floor were ordered turned down, this curfew meant "lights out" at midnight. Bowling alleys and billiard parlors, dance halls and cabarets, and all of New York City's restaurants were affected. Hotels like the Essex House would take the last cocktail order at their elegant Casino-in-the-Park at 11:45. For Horn & Hardart, functioning through a war was not new. In 1918, with troops overseas, the cafeterias and Automats had experienced "wheatless, heatless, and meatless" days. Wheatless bread recipes were featured in newspapers and called Liberty Bread. Horn & Hardart was also forced to allot just one teaspoon of sugar per customer. Now another World War was calling on the country to make sacrifices.

In the midst of this darkness, a light note was sounded on the first night of curfew at the Horn & Hardart on Times Square: Following the regular performance of their musical *Laffing Room Only,* actress Betty Garrett, the comedy team of Olsen and Johnson, and the show's entire cast walked the five blocks from Broadway's Winter Garden Theatre to the Automat, where they performed a selection of scenes from the show.

A month before the city's curfew, Mayor La Guardia announced that Tuesdays and Fridays would be "meatless": butchers could not sell meat and restaurants could not serve it. The pitch-in-and-help spirit was not lost on New York City. Almost immediately, some of the city's leading chefs began putting together a booklet containing two thousand meatless dishes. Childs, another of the city's restaurant chains, saluted the mayor's Italian heritage with pasta e faggioli, a dish whose main ingredients were macaroni and kidney beans. Schrafft's served a chickenless vegetable à la king at their restaurants. As for Horn & Hardart, since there were no war restrictions on animal organs or innards, their commissary came up with tripe creole and kidney stew. In a letter to his son, Gus Jr., a lieutenant in the Marines in 1945, Gus Sr., vice-president of the company, wrote: "We are selling a lot of the junk that you like, such as liver, kidney stew, and tripe. We still have the old standbys like Hamburger, Chopped Steak, Beaf Pie, Baked Ham but not so often."

Dr. Aaron Rausen remembers how as an eleven-year-old he discovered that the country was at war at the Automat on 181st Street: "This was a Sunday and it was exceptionally noisy, and it seemed to be more frenetic than I had ever recalled. I asked what was happening. Everyone seemed to be running around. My recollection was that a tall Coast Guardsman said, 'Have you heard they bombed Pearl Harbor?' I wasn't quite sure what Pearl Harbor was and I don't think many people did."

At the beginning of 1942, red, white, and blue placards were placed in all Horn & Hardart Automats and cafeterias, reminding customers that sugar was a vital commodity and should be used sparingly. The government issued price ceilings: No restaurant could charge more for items like coffee, bacon and eggs, and roast beef than what the government stipulated (unless their regular prices had been higher before October 1942).

As the war went on and more men were drafted, countermen were replaced by women, some of whom worked until midnight. This was a change for Horn & Hardart, whose rules did not permit women to work later than ten. Their retail shops, which had grown in New York City from ten in 1931 to seventeen by 1943, changed their closing hours from 8:00 P.M. to 6:30 P.M. And by the summer of 1944, Horn & Hardart had hired hundreds of schoolchildren who wanted to work during their vacation.

That year the company operated with fewer employees than in any one year from 1930 through 1940. "We're very short of help, since the schoolchildren left us," Gus Hardart Sr. wrote to his son. Among the employees' added duties was keeping an eye on the flatware, which was leaving the Automats at an alarming rate. As part of the war effort, manufacturing restrictions were placed on metal. Spoons, knives, and forks, which could be easily fenced, seemed to have legs. Another item that sometimes "walked" out of the Automats was butter, which was heavily rationed. One day Gus Hardart caught an employee taking butter patties and stuffing them into his hat.

Instead of firing him on the spot, Hardart followed the man outside and engaged him in conversation, chatting with him until the butter melted and began dripping down the man's face. Two Automats were shut down: one on Thirty-seventh Street and Broadway and another in the Bronx, at East 170th Street.

In an effort to maintain efficiency with fewer employees, Horn & Hardart placed rails along all of the steam counters so people would be forced to form a line rather than serendipitously approach the counter, as had always been the case. "Our stores at lunch hour resemble the subway rush in the evening," wrote Gus Hardart Sr. There was also a cashier at the end of the line, relieving the women behind the steam tables whose jobs also entailed taking money. This invention arose out of necessity, but it pleased customers immensely and remained part of the way the Automat-cafeterias operated. But this was the only smile that Horn & Hardart could put on its customers' faces. A 1945 stockholders report emphasized the short supply of food—sometimes so acute that menu items had to be eliminated—the shortage of help, and the impossibility of planning for a future that was still uncertain.

In spite of the war, life went on. In the 1930s and into the 1940s, bandleader Fred Waring held a weekly luncheon for songwriters at the Automat on Broadway and Fifty-fifth Street, not far from the Brill Building, where many songwriters worked. Waring and his Pennsylvanians entertained New Yorkers five nights a week on *Pleasure Time,* their popular radio show. Sitting at one of the Automat's rear tables, behind a special cake that the Automat baked for five dollars, Waring held court while song publishers brought him their latest ditties. These weekly sessions became known as "Fred's Automatinees."

The Automat's familiarity became part of the mortar that held people together. In a *New York* magazine article, playwright Neil Simon wrote of growing up during the war years: "Into the forties, I maintained my affection for the Automat. Hours spent doing my homework over milk and cupcakes (same taste, slightly higher price), and the same friendly but unrequested conversation: 'What are you, a youngster?' 'What do you think of this war? Some crazy business, huh?'"

From top: Truck drivers during union negotiations. Behind the glass doors. Art Deco at its best, New York City Automat.

I found my first full-time job working for the Metropolitan Museum of Art. I was paid the enormous salary of $33 a week. I made sandwiches to take to my job, and then in the evening, lo and behold, there was this magical Horn & Hardart, this huge Horn & Hardart on East Eighty-sixth Street between Lexington and Third. One of my big treats was going to the Automat for dinner. For maybe $1.50 or $1.75, I could have a dish of very, very tasty food. At least I had one nourishing meal a day. This was a lifesaver. It helped me through the week.

BERNARD WOLF, Photographer and Author

There was a sad note for Horn & Hardart, unrelated to the war. On October 13, 1941, eighty-year-old Joseph Horn died; he had sat each day at Philadelphia's Sample Table until the last year of his life. Thirty-five hundred employees from Philadelphia and five hundred from New York City filed past his bier. Edwin Daly, a man who worked closely with Horn for eleven years and had been acting president of the New York company since 1936, now took the reins in New York City and Philadelphia. There would be some choppy waters ahead for Daly and Horn & Hardart. Once he got past the food and staff shortages of the war years, the new president would find a country emerging from that war in a very different state of mind.

In September 1946, the nickel glass of milk vanished from Horn & Hardart. Now it would cost ten cents to fill an 8½-ounce glass with homogenized milk. By 1947, Horn & Hardart caught up with the unionized chains and initiated a forty-hour work-week. Although the move was an expensive one, the company, which had relied on immigrants willing to work cheaply, knew it had no choice. After the war, the cost of food had risen sharply and the minimum wage rose from forty to sixty cents per hour. By 1948, Horn & Hardart's letter to its New York stockholders, issued by Daly, was brimming with optimism. The boys were coming home, and six hundred of them had already returned to their jobs at Horn & Hardart. "Business is good, exceptionally good," Daly wrote, anticipating the construction of new buildings. Already, there were three new retail stores: two in Forest Hills, Queens, and one in Pennsylvania Station.

With the war a thing of the past, everyone thought there was nowhere to look now but up. What Daly and most business leaders did not factor in was the war's psychological impact. Old institutions, everything from restaurants to railroads, were no longer cherished. For Horn & Hardart, the restaurant chain that accompanied so many through a Depression and this all-too-recent war, its days as a vibrant part of the cityscape were numbered.

Opposite: Trinity Place, New York City.

We're All Family

I spent so much time in Horn & Hardart's, it's incredible. I think about it often, oddly enough, because it was such a great time in my life. I can't think of anything that was not great at the Automat. I wish they were still around.

JAMES DARREN

In December 1927, Joe Horn decided to play Santa Claus. The married but childless Horn gave a Christmas party for all of the employees' children in New York and Philadelphia, making sure each left with a gift. The parties became a tradition, and by 1939 two separate parties were given in Philadelphia's Broadwood Hotel to accommodate fifteen hundred children. After cake and sodas and a vaudeville show, Santa Claus, accompanied by twenty employees dressed as storybook characters, distributed gifts. Through the years, the parties got more elaborate. By 1953, the New York company booked the Hotel Astor's Grand Ballroom.

Opposite: The Horn & Hardart clan at the annual Christmas party. Above: A brochure to recruit employees.

Every employee knew that when those children grew up, they could find jobs with the company waiting for them. Some families had three generations of Horn & Hardart employees, all part of what Joe Horn liked to think of as the family business. And once someone joined "the family," he or she was often in it for life.

Tony Voell, hired in 1888 by Frank Hardart, was considered the company's first employee when he began at the Chestnut Street lunchroom in Philadelphia; Voell was still working for Horn & Hardart in New York City in the 1950s.

In a 1953 issue of the *Horn & Hardart Herald* (the New York company newspaper), shipper Sam Stitch, who joined Horn & Hardart in 1918, glowed over his thirty-five-year stint: "I was originally hired as a machineman. From then on out the world was my oyster. Coffeeman, head bus, cashier, P.M. manager, etc. etc. After three years of this I was transferred to the commissary, and have been there ever since." Stitch's aunt Clara, who worked at the original Times Square Horn & Hardart, remembered serving cofounder Frank Hardart and his wife, Mary. Stitch himself came in contact with Horn & Hardart vice-president Augustin Hardart Sr. when the company practical joker, known to feign passing out at the Sample Table, twice pulled April Fools' jokes on him. "Out of the truck jumped a figure that resembled a tiger or a wolf,"

Stitch wrote, describing one of Hardart's stunts when he leaped from a delivery truck in an animal costume. Another time, Hardart disguised himself as an Englishman, intentionally annoying Stitch while pretending to observe him at work. Only when the exasperated shipper was about to blow his top did Hardart remove his hat and mustache and exclaim, "April Fool, Sam."

Camaraderie between management and employees was rare in the forties and fifties, especially in a large firm where workers' duties were always routine and often menial. At Horn & Hardart, managers came up from the ranks, often starting as busboys. Tom Gibbons, the company's president during its dark days in the 1970s, started working at Horn & Hardart at sixteen as a seventy-two-cent-an-hour busboy. In true apprentice fashion, he moved on to porter, dishwasher, coffeeman, counterman, griddleman, food checker, cashier, and finally nickel thrower, where he had the distinction of being the only male at that job. While their father served as president, Gibbons's three sons worked for the company as day, night, and relief managers. Joseph A. Horn, the founder's grand-nephew, became secretary of the Philadelphia company, but not without first climbing his own ladder: from busboy to assistant manager, taking four more positions before his appointment to secretary sixteen years later. The company brass was such a family affair that in 1937, at its forty-ninth anniversary dinner, half of the twelve executives who attended were related.

Even employees who didn't make Horn & Hardart a career often left with lasting memories. In Sally Alessandroni Downey's case, those

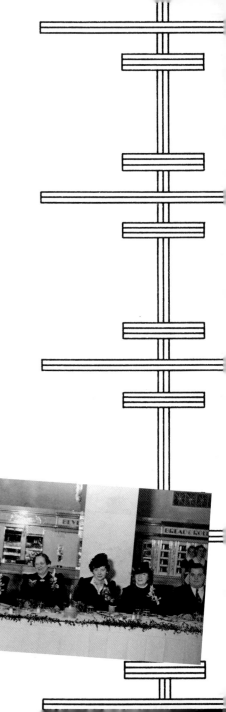

Gus Hardart III tells Santa his Christmas wishes.

memories are especially dear. Downey, a native Philadelphian, met her future husband when both worked at the Automat. "Marriages between H & H employees were common," Downey explained in an article she wrote for the *Philadelphia Inquirer,* "but ours was one of the few wedding receptions that the company catered." The guests dined on baked ham, chicken salad, and a wedding cake baked in the commissary, served by waitresses whose yellow aprons and handkerchiefs perfectly matched the bridesmaids' gowns.

The sense of company-as-family was fostered by Joe Horn, whose pride in the company was very personal. In a 1954 *Saturday Evening Post* article, Jack Alexander wrote: "Short of committing a felony, it is well-nigh impossible for an H & H employee to get fired. It is almost as difficult to resign." According to Alexander, Horn would encourage employees to "bring their troubles, business or private, to him personally and he reveled in helping them out with advice or financial help."

The private problems a personnel manager might handle ranged from offering a transfer to someone who found a co-worker intolerable to advice to the lovelorn. In his article, Alexander cites one: "A woman working in the bakery falls in love with a baker and wants to marry him. The baker, who is married and has a family, refuses. The woman turns in her resignation, life being no longer worthwhile. The personnel man hears her out, sympathizes with her trouble of the heart, and suggests a transfer to another division of the plant. She turns it down, but agrees that after a few weeks of resting at home, she may come back and accept the transfer."

For problems of a more practical nature, Joe Horn set up a private foundation, which had grown to four hundred thousand dollars at the time of his death. Interest-free loans were granted for overdue bills ranging from late mortgage payments to installments on television sets. And since the company did not have a hospital insurance plan or built-in sick days, it wasn't unusual for the foundation to pick up the cost of an operation and sometimes convalescence time.

There was free group life insurance and disability coverage, and a modest pension plan that supplemented Social Security. And all employees got an annual Christmas bonus based on their salary and years of service. The bonus started at 2 percent for one year of service, continuing to 8 percent for employees who had been with the company for twenty years. Even in 1935, when the Depression was deeply entrenched, Horn & Hardart paid out a quarter of a million dollars in Christmas bonuses. The company also provided free meals during working hours and a 25 percent discount at their retail shops. During the Depression years, those free meals compensated for the meager quarter-an-hour wages. Employees who had college-age children were eligible to compete for the annual twenty-plus scholarships that Joe Horn gave out. And those who worked at Horn & Hardart for a quarter of a century became members of the 25-Year Club: Along with gold watches and diamond-studded service pins, members were entitled to four-week vacations.

Even with its low wages and few paid holidays, Horn & Hardart was able to resist any major unionizing attempts until 1955, when the Teamsters waged a violent and sometimes bloody fight against the Philadelphia company. Intimidation tactics included the trashing and burning of trucks; one was even dumped in the river. The employees rejected that unionizing attempt, as well as two others in the early 1960s, involving commissary workers. It wasn't until 1967 that the AFL-CIO won a thirty-year battle, enrolling Philadelphia's Horn & Hardart workers in the Hotel, Restaurant, and Bartenders Union.

One factor that made Joe Horn's benevolent despotism palatable for so long was the ethnicity of the company. Horn & Hardart was, for all intents, a company of Irish Roman Catholics. Although many of the Philadelphia hierarchy were Masons, much of the Hardart family was Irish and Catholic, as was Edwin Daly, who succeeded Joe Horn as president. In Philadelphia, it was once joked that Irish immigrants coming off the boat would head straight to Horn & Hardart for a job. Paul Downey's uncle, grandfather, and cousin all worked for Horn & Hardart, and they were all Irish immigrants. "Irish Catholics were available when the company went through its greatest period of expansion," says Downey. "It was really a Depression baby."

It was such a clan that in 1949 the company began holding annual Communion Breakfasts in Philadelphia and New York City for employees. Presiding over their eighth breakfast in New York City was permanent toastmaster Thomas Hardart, cofounder Frank Hardart's grandson. After mass, the employees would gather for breakfast at the large flagship Horn & Hardart on Trinity Place. By 1951, when Ed Daly was president, the New York City breakfast moved uptown, to the Hotel Astor on Times Square. There was also a dietary concession to its Catholic customers: During Lent, oyster pie was added to the menu.

But black Americans who were hired by Horn & Hardart were kept behind the scenes, usually as chefs. "There wasn't much chance for a black cook to advance to management in those days, but there were bonuses at Christmas, and a kind of family feeling," said retired chef Leon J. Grimes, who worked for Horn & Hardart for thirty-seven years. "Through the 1950s, racial prejudice was so deep that blacks were not allowed to be seen handling food," says Paul Downey. It wasn't until the 1960s that a black counterwoman was made a waitress, and she was given that job because of pressure from the NAACP.

The sense of family that kept employees in the company, even when they knew the money wasn't all that good, extended beyond working hours. In the 1930s, both

When we were growing up, our big thing was to come into the city for the Christmas Show or the Easter Show at Radio City Music Hall. I had three sisters and four cousins. Part of the day in the city was to go to the Automat. We went and got four nickels and then got our food. They had a little yellow cupcake, upside down with some kind of decorations on top. That was the best. Part of the fun was to try to catch a peak behind those windows to see if anyone was there.

JOHN HARNEY, COO and Vice-President, NYU Hospitals Center

the Philadelphia and New York City companies had bowling teams: the Philadelphia Phils and the New York Hustlers. The teams often met at Phil's Recreation Center, over the Automat at 1167 Sixth Avenue, and competed annually for the Joseph V. Horn Bowling Trophy. Everyone got to read the scores in the *Horn & Hardart Herald*, along with marriage, birth, and death announcements. And when an employee died, no matter how menial his or her job, the grieving family knew that the president and other officers would be at the funeral parlor to pay their respects.

For the immigrants who worked at Horn & Hardart, there was also the sense of connection to a beloved American institution that was loved. For doorman Steve Keschi, it was his first job. "I came to this country from Hungary on a Saturday, and Horn & Hardart hired me on a Tuesday. I loved it. I didn't speak a word of English. There was a German girl making salads. When customers asked me for something, she translated in German what I should make." These immigrants were serving the sons and daughters of people who had been in their shoes, and it made them feel hopeful and proud. They were an integral part of the country.

I worked for them for almost twenty years. I loved it. I worked in the one on Fifty-seventh Street the longest. We had a doctor who liked to drop in every day. I'd turn the chair over so no one would sit on it. People would come in and say, "What's the matter with that seat?" I'd say, "It's reserved." "Reserved?" they'd say. "For who?" He was a nice doctor.

MOLLY COPPOLA, **Former Employee**

Oatmeal Cookies

makes about 36

⅔ cup oatmeal

½ cup raisins

½ cup vegetable shortening

1 cup sugar

¼ teaspoon baking soda

½ teaspoon cinnamon

¼ teaspoon salt

2 cups all-purpose flour

2 tablespoons whole milk

1 large egg

Preheat the oven to 375°F.

In a food processor, grind the oatmeal with the raisins for 2 minutes. In an electric mixer, blend the shortening and sugar until light and fluffy. Beat in the baking soda, cinnamon, and salt until mixed. Stir in the flour, the oatmeal-raisin mixture, milk, and the egg. Beat at high speed for 2 minutes, until the mixture is smooth.

Drop the mixture by rounded tablespoonfuls, 2 inches apart, onto an ungreased cookie sheet. Bake 10 to 12 minutes, until lightly browned. With a metal spatula, remove the cookies to wire racks to cool. Repeat with the remaining dough. Store the cookies in a tightly covered container.

Opposite: Herald Square, New York City, 1936.

Mashed Potatoes

serves 6

6 medium Idaho potatoes (about 2 pounds), peeled

4 tablespoons (½ stick) unsalted butter

1 teaspoon salt

¼ teaspoon freshly ground white pepper

¾ cup milk, at room temperature

In a 3-quart saucepan over high heat, heat the potatoes and enough water to cover them to boiling. Reduce the heat to low and simmer approximately 30 minutes, or until fork-tender. Drain in a colander and allow the potatoes to sit for 2 minutes, to dry completely.

In an electric mixer at low speed, blend the potatoes, butter, salt, and pepper for 1 to 2 minutes, until the potatoes are completely broken up. Add the milk gradually while whipping. Whip at high speed for 1 to 2 minutes, until the potatoes are light and fluffy.

The Horn & Hardart Children's Hour

Good morning. The Horn & Hardart Automat, Cafeterias, and Less-Work-for-Mother Retail Shops present New York's most talented children in a full-hour variety program for the entertainment of adults as well as boys and girls.

VOICE OF HOST ED HERLIHY,
June 18, 1944

One story goes that in 1928, Alice Clements, wife of the man whose advertising agency handled the Horn & Hardart Baking Company, was passing by a children's playroom in the McClatchy's Shopping Center in Philadelphia. She noticed how engaged the children were with some toy microphones, entertaining themselves with impromptu routines. It was at this point that the idea hit her: Why not produce a children's show for radio on which the children would do the entertaining?

Opposite: Stan Lee Broza (far left) hosting The Horn & Hardart Children's Hour on WCAU radio in Philadelphia. Above: The *Stars of Tomorrow* newsletter.

Then there's the other story: One day in 1927, Stan Lee Broza, part owner and vice-president in charge of programming at radio station WCAU in Philadelphia, had also visited that same playroom. He too observed how absorbed the children were as they sang and organized games. In his biography, Broza claims that *The Children's Hour* was originally a neighborhood project for the shopping center. "They [Horn & Hardart] wanted me to do a short commercial campaign for it," Broza said.

While the who-was-there-first debate was going on, *The Horn & Hardart Children's Hour,* one of the most successful shows of its kind, was born. In Philadelphia, *The Children's Hour* was hosted by Broza and written and produced by his wife, Esther. It began as a radio show on WCAU, and in 1948, with the arrival of television, it was broadcast on WCAU-TV's Channel 10 from studios in Philadelphia. In New York City, Alice Clements wrote, produced, and directed *The Children's Hour,* airing it on WABC-radio and later on WNBC-TV. She hired actor Paul Douglas as the first host. Ralph Edwards succeeded Douglas, who went on to a Hollywood film career. When Edwards left in 1940, Ed Herlihy took over.

According to a 1943 *Time* article, Joe Horn balked at Clements's suggestion, even though the Philadelphia *Children's Hour* had gotten Horn & Hardart's go-ahead. "We don't want to put a lot of squeaky brats on the air!" he reportedly said. And Ike Clements, Alice's husband and the head of Horn & Hardart's advertising company, supposedly wasn't sold on the idea either. It was Clements's agency that came up with the slogan "Less Work for Mother" when Horn & Hardart decided to launch its retail shops; they also coined "The finest possible quality at the lowest possible prices." It wasn't until a trial show, when Horn & Hardart's cash registers began ringing louder, that the New York show supposedly got the green light.

The Horn & Hardart Children's Hour became a defining part of Alice Clements's life. Born in Pennsylvania coal country, the starstruck Alice Viola Weast enrolled in New York City's American Academy of Dramatic Arts, studied ballet, and had a few turns on the stage (limited to the chorus) before marrying Ike Clements. Alice conceived twins who were stillborn, and for the couple there would be no more children. *The Horn & Hardart Children's Hour,* which would become one of the longest-running shows on radio and television, would consume her days for the next thirty years.

Every week she would travel to New York City and on Fridays set up shop in a studio in Radio City Music Hall. There, she would audition from fifty to seventy children. "Oh, she was wonderful," remembers Edith Dickstein, who as Edith Shuster sang and tap-danced in 1936, when the show was aired on WABC-radio. "I was the Cheer-Up Girl," says Dickstein, who was ten years old when she tap-danced to "East Side, West Side," the show's theme song. The show was so popular that Horn & Hardart issued a weekly radio guide advertising their retail shops' specials, which in 1938 included two chicken croquettes and a half-pound of lima beans for thirty cents. As of 1943, more than one hundred thousand children auditioned for Aunt Alice, as she became known. Tap-dancers, jugglers, baton-twirlers, and singers showed up with their mothers for a shot on the Sunday-morning show.

"I sang 'Please Don't Let the Birdies Die.' It was a song Alice Clements asked me to sing," says Bernadette Peters, who was five years old when she appeared on *The Children's Hour.* "The great thing about those days was that it was live," says Peters. "To me, it was just playacting. They put me in the spot and I sang. I didn't know I was on television." Peters remembers appearing on the show three times, once singing "Hard-Hearted Hannah" and another time appearing as Brunhilda. "They put muffin tins on me and they had to butter up the tins because they reflected in the camera," says Peters. One story, told by the late Ed Herlihy, recalls one little girl crying on the set because she was playing the death scene from *The Little Match Girl.* Apparently, she thought that like her character she was really going to die.

Even children who didn't make show business their career got to have their moment in the spotlight. Maureen Gillespie was invited on the show with her entire dance class. "I got ten dollars, a fruitcake in a tin, and a brown attaché case with my name engraved in gold letters. Imagine being an eight-year-old walking around with an engraved attaché case. I always claim *The Horn & Hardart Children's Hour* was my first paying job in show business." Others, like Leida Snow, adviser to Congressman Jerrold Nadler, who danced on the show several times, have less romantic memories. "I remember that they never fed us. They would pick us up very, very early in the morning, when it was still dark. Hours would go by with no food." In desperation, the five-year-old began to eat the set. "The set was dressed to show Horn & Hardart products, and I remember one day taking some bites. My mother was concerned because she thought they might have doctored the food to make it look good."

For a time, the Hoffman Beverage Company cosponsored the show in New York. According to Bernadette Peters, children who appeared were given hatboxes filled with small bottles of Hoffman soda. But it was Horn & Hardart that gave the variety show its caché, so much so that in 1943, Alice Clements was grooming Bobby Hookey, one of the regulars, for a role in a children's musical comedy she hoped to produce called *Automatically Yours*. She had also decided to mold him into a teenage heart-throb, presenting him each week with a new love interest. "Bobby Hookey and Kenny Best did an act together," says Nancy Herbert, who was eleven or twelve when she watched the show faithfully every Sunday morning. Kenny Best went to Herbert's camp. "My friend Meryl and I each had wild crushes on him," says Herbert, whose camp counselor was Marsha Gustin, another *Children's Hour* star, who played Brooklyn in an ongoing comedy duet, *Brooklyn and Bronxie*. Another regular whom Herbert remembers was a large blind girl who sang the jingle, "Less Work for Mother." That jingle, with lyrics by Elizabeth Masterman Zindel (credited with creating the first singing jingle, for dog food), was on every viewer's lips.

Less work for mother; let's lend her a hand.
Less work for mother so she'll understand.
She's your greatest treasure; let's make her life a pleasure.
Less work for mother dear.

Clockwise from left: Performers on *The Horn & Hardart Children's Hour*; Bill Curtis, Ed Herlihy, and Marlebone at Horn & Hardart opening in Wanamaker's department store, Westchester, New York. Edith Shuster doing her skit.

Alice Clements with Ed Herlihy and the *Children's Hour* gang, 1940.

Alice Clements, the woman once described as a "sleek, soft-spoken, sophisticated lady," threw all of her own show-business ambitions into *The Children's Hour*. According to Ralph Edwards, she was a good businesswoman with a great insight into show business. In 1950, just when the show was being launched on television, her husband died, and Alice took over the advertising agency while still running the show. According to Ed Herlihy's widow, she taught Ed how to dance so he could do skits with the children. She even combed through burlesque shows for material she could adapt.

In Philadelphia, Stan Lee Broza turned *The Children's Hour* into an outlet for the talented underprivileged of South Philly. Like Alice Clements, Esther Broza had been bitten by show business. Before marrying, she had made a name for herself in several amateur productions. When she and Stan Lee, a former soap salesman, started *The Children's Hour*, they put their hearts into it, encouraging the neighborhood children to try out. "I was taken to audition on a Saturday, and the following day I was on the show," says singer Kitty Kallen, who became a regular in 1936. "They were very proud of me," says Kallen, who got other bookings because of the Brozas. "I used to be called Philadelphia's Judy Garland." Kallen, whose 1954 hit "Little Things Mean a Lot" was on the top of the charts, credits the Brozas with jump-starting her career. By the time she was nine, the little girl from South Philly was doing vaudeville and making 350 dollars a week.

Several of the performers on *The Children's Hour* in Philadelphia went on to very successful careers. "The Brozas gave me my first chance," said singer/actor Frankie Avalon in an interview with *Cosmopolitan*. Avalon, who lived on South Thirteenth Street, flunked nine auditions before he was finally put on the show. Eddie Fisher, who was also on the show, was so poor his family sometimes had to go on welfare. Bobby Rydell also got his start with the Brozas. So did Ezra Stone, who was the cracking-voiced son Henry Aldrich on radio's *The Aldrich Family.* And the famous tap-dancing Nicholas Brothers began their careers on *The Children's Hour* as well. Besides Bernadette Peters, comedian Arnold Stang and television personality Robert Q. Lewis were on the New York show. Comedienne Madeline Kahn was on *The Children's Hour,* as was actress Ann Sothern.

The Horn & Hardart Children's Hour in New York and Philadelphia entered people's living rooms into the late fifties. By then, however, the show's audience—children who enjoyed watching their contemporaries perform—had grown up. The new generation of children wasn't interested in variety shows. Their tastes were leaning to adventure yarns like *Sergeant Preston of the Yukon* and the British-made *Adventures of Robin Hood.* Animated cartoons would become weekend fare with the introduction of *The Mighty Mouse Playhouse*—the first animated cartoon series, which debuted on Saturday-morning network television in 1955.

On July 9, 1958, a small item appeared in a Philadelphia newspaper announcing the suspension of *The Children's Hour* on WCAU-TV for the first time in thirty years. Esther Broza put on a good face, telling the reporter that she and Stan Lee had been wanting to take a summer off. They said they hoped to resume the program in September with another sponsor. But for both New York City and Philadelphia, without Horn & Hardart, there would be no more *Children's Hour.*

When our children were little we would take them to the Macy's Thanksgiving Day Parade, and after the parade, we would go to the Horn & Hardart on Fifty-seventh Street for some hot chocolate. It was warm and you could afford it. And the kids always looked forward to it.

BRIDI DOINO, Manager, Monro Wines and Spirits

Chicken Potpie

serves 6

1 chicken (3 to 4 pounds)

1 medium yellow onion, roughly chopped

3 ribs celery, roughly chopped

1 teaspoon salt

1 teaspoon freshly ground white pepper

1 cup frozen peas

2 medium potatoes, peeled and cut into ½-inch dice

2 medium carrots, peeled and cut into ½-inch dice

4 tablespoons vegetable oil

4 tablespoons all-purpose flour

½ teaspoon celery salt

2 cubes chicken bouillon

1 9-inch prepared pastry crust, about ¼ inch thick

1 egg yolk

Rinse the chicken with running cold water. Place the chicken, onion, celery, salt, ½ teaspoon of the pepper, and enough water to cover in an 8-quart saucepot. Bring to a boil, then reduce the heat to low, cover, and simmer about 1½ hours, or until the chicken is fork-tender. Reserve 3 cups of the broth, and remove the chicken to a large bowl; refrigerate for 30 minutes, or until cool enough to handle. Discard the skin and bones from chicken, and cut the meat into bite-sized pieces.

Preheat the oven to 400°F.

Cook the peas according to package directions. Drain and set aside.

In a 3-quart saucepan over high flame, heat the potatoes, carrots, and enough water to cover them. Bring to a boil, reduce the heat to low, and simmer for 15 minutes, or until the vegetables are fork-tender. Drain and set aside.

In 1-quart saucepan, bring the reserved broth to a boil. Remove from the heat. In a separate saucepan over low heat, blend the oil and flour. Stirring constantly, cook for 2 to 3 minutes, until the mixture is smooth and golden brown. Continue to stir and gradually add the hot broth; cook 5 to 8 minutes, until thickened. Add the remaining ½ teaspoon pepper, celery salt, and chicken bouillon. Remove from the heat.

In a large bowl, combine the chicken pieces with the gravy and the reserved vegetables. Pour the mixture into a 2½-quart casserole dish. Place the pastry crust loosely over the chicken mixture. Trim the pastry edge, leaving a 1-inch overhang; fold the overhang under and press gently all around casserole dish to make a high stand-up edge.

In a cup, beat the egg yolk with 1 teaspoon of water. Brush the pastry with the egg yolk mixture. Bake in the preheated oven for 20 to 30 minutes, or until the crust is well browned.

HORN & HARDART
on STAGE and SCREEN

A kiss may be grand, but it won't pay the rental
On your humble flat, or help you at the Automat.

JULE STYNE,
"Diamonds Are a Girl's Best Friend"

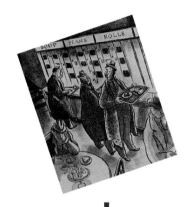

It didn't take Hollywood long to discover the Automat. In 1925, the silent film *The Beautiful City* featured William Powell as a gangster who robs an Automat of its nickels. Broadway celebrated the Automat extravagantly in 1932, with Moss Hart's Depression-themed musical *Face the Music*. Hart had already mentioned the Automat in the script of his first Broadway play, the 1930 hit *Once in a Lifetime*. But *Face the Music* used the Automat as ground zero for the city's hard times. With music and lyrics by Irving Berlin, the play depicts the down-on-their-heels

Opposite: Coleen Gray and Richard Conte in *The Sleeping City*, 1950. Above: *New York Evening Post* cartoon.

rich forced to abandon their table linens for nickel meals at Horn & Hardart. Both the first and second acts have scenes that take place there, and Berlin wrote two Automat songs for the show: the first, "Lunching at the Automat," also known as "The Automat Song," and the more famous "Let's Have Another Cup of Coffee," which became a Depression anthem. It might have been Berlin's own experience with his daughter at the Automat that became his inspiration. In her book, *Irving Berlin: A Daughter's Memoir,* Mary Ellin Barrett writes of jaunts in the city with her father: "Maybe he walked me up Sixth Avenue to the Horn & Hardart on Fifty-seventh Street. Certainly one of my earliest memories is of the two of us at the Automat, he enjoying as much as I did putting in a nickel and extracting a piece of pie."

Back in Hollywood, the Depression spawned three more movies with scenes shot in the Automat. Not surprisingly, each featured hungry heroines. In 1934, Joan Crawford was the title character in *Sadie McKee,* an impecunious working girl who longs for the dinner in which her indifferent tablemate is about to bury his cigarette. That same year, Preston Sturges cowrote *Thirty Day Princess,* a comedy that featured Sylvia Sidney and Cary Grant. Sidney, who plays a dual role of a princess and an unemployed actress, is seen banging on one of the Automat's vending doors, trying to get at the dinner inside. Another Preston Sturges film, the 1937 *Easy Living,* features Ray Milland as an Automat worker who slips hungry Jean Arthur a beef pie. Sturges

uses the vending-machine doors for slapstick: When Milland trips a "secret lever," releasing the doors, he precipitates a free-for-all as food is flung at unsuspecting faces.

Into the 1960s, Hollywood's hungry heroines found themselves at the Automat. In *That Touch of Mink* (1962) it's Doris Day's turn to stand in

Left: Doris Day in *That Touch of Mink,* 1962.
Opposite: Victor Mature and Jean Simmons in *Affair with a Stranger,* 1953.

front of a vending machine, waiting for her pal Audrey Meadows to slip her some food. Woody Allen turned it into memory in his 1987 nostalgia-driven film, *Radio Days*. The young Brooklyn-bred Allen character, who is a child of the 1930s, is taken to Manhattan where he is treated to a show at Radio City Music Hall and dinner at the Automat. As recently as 2001, the Automat was featured in two Broadway revivals: *Bells Are Ringing,* opened with a

film montage that includes customers in front of a vending machine, reaching for their food. In *42nd Street,* the Automat is mentioned and appears among familiar Times Square marquees on scenery.

The Automat became a perfect backdrop for publicity shots. Everything from model shoots for fashion magazines to the occasional paparazzi snap of celebrities catching a meal made it into print. Movie star Rudy Vallee, who claimed an aversion to tipping, was photographed pouring his own coffee in front of a dolphin-headed spout. Another star of the 1930s, Mexican-born Ramon Novarro, had a special reason for getting his picture taken at Horn & Hardart: In 1918, he worked at one of the Automats as a busboy. In a 1937 column, Walter Winchell couldn't resist giving a spin to actress Veronica Lake's first visit to the Automat. Winchell related how a group of women, standing behind this sultry blonde, couldn't resist berating her for trying to look like a certain movie star. In a reverse turn, Horn & Hardart hired the comedy team of Abbott and Costello in 1939 to promote their Christmas fruitcake. The ad, showing the pair doing battle over a tinned cake, appeared in local newspapers.

Parties at Automats became a great publicity gimmick. When 20th Century-Fox released its film *Our Man Flint* in 1966, a 4 A.M. screening was followed by a special champagne breakfast at a nearby Automat. In a publicity shot, a guest in top hat and tails stood with his date before a wall of vending machines. A hand is seen coming

Clockwise from top left: Victor Mature approaching Jean Simmons in *Affair with a Stranger*, 1953; one of many fashion shots using the Automat; Jack Benny with Kokomo at his Automat party for 500 friends, 1960; Jean Arthur in *Easy Living*, 1937; Peter Lawford and Janet Leigh in *Just This Once*, 1952; models in a Brazilian magazine, 1966; Robert Young and Ruth Hussey in *Married Bachelor*, 1941; Virginia Welles and Eddie Bracken in *Ladies' Man*, 1946.

through one of the slots usually reserved for pies and sandwiches, pouring champagne into Horn & Hardart paper cups. In 1968, when comedian Pat Paulsen decided to make a tongue-in-cheek run for president, he held an eighty-nine-cents-a-plate fund-raising dinner at the Fifty-seventh Street Automat. Tom Smothers, Soupy Sales, Steve Lawrence, and Eydie Gormé were among the celebrities who attended.

The best publicity party of all was given on November 10, 1960, by Jack Benny at the Automat on Forty-second Street and Third Avenue. Benny was about to launch a new television season, and his guests—most of whom arrived by limousine—included Helen Hayes, Polly Bergen, Audrey Meadows, Celeste Holm, William Inge, Jack Lemmon, Rosalind Russell, Ed Sullivan, Hume Cronyn, and Jessica Tandy. In keeping with his "cheap-skate" image, Benny stood in the cashier's booth and pre-sented each of his gowned and tuxedoed guests with a two-dollar roll of nickels. "He told a couple of funny sto-ries that night," said Joe Franklin, who was one of the guests. "He said he was giving another violin concert. He was charging two dollars to sit up front and one hundred dollars to sit in the back." The party really delivered for Benny, who read about himself in several newspapers, including the *London Daily Express*.

Artists, writers, photographers, and cartoonists all found inspiration at the Automat. In 1927, Edward Hopper painted a woman alone at a table with a cup of coffee and titled it *Automat*. Berenice Abbott's black-and-white photo of a man stand-

Above: Chef Francis Bourdon in the *New York Daily News*, 1967. Right: *Seventeen* magazine, 1948.

ing before a wall of vending machines at the Eighth Avenue Automat is a classic. Illustrators put the Automat on magazine covers, including a 1938 *New Yorker* that shows a chauffeur waiting patiently as two children put their nickels in the slots. And inside those magazines and in many newspapers, cartoonists from Peter Arno to Al Hirschfeld had something to say about the Automat. In the funnies, The Little King, Winnie Winkle, Brenda Breeze, and Mutt and Jeff each had a moment at the Automat. Even Donald Duck got into the Automat act in a four-panel cartoon appearing in the *New York Evening Journal* on September 20, 1944.

The charm of the Automat was not lost on writers. In his 1930 informal guidebook to New York City, French-born Paul Morand described lunch at an "automatic" restaurant:

They are delightful, these bars with their devices for dealing out change in nickels, where everybody walks about with his own tray, the collisions, the soup you receive down your neck, the smiles of the girls at the serving-counter, like fair hospital nurses, the gathering of all the ordinary people of the sidewalks. Here sits the policeman whose turn of duty is over, laying his now useless baton on the table, here the shy young vegetarian looking like Lindbergh, here the negress as shiny as her shoes, and the typist who has not yet had a present of pearls from her employer. I have a great weakness for the common folk of America—there are none more delightful.

Betty Smith's 1943 best-seller, *A Tree Grows in Brooklyn,* uses the Automat as a mark of youthful emancipation:

And Neely ate in a restaurant. Like Francie, he had brought his lunch the first day but the boys made fun of him, calling him the country boy from Brooklyn. After that, Mama gave him fifteen cents a day for lunch. He told Francie how he ate in a place called the Automat where you could put a nickel in a slot and coffee and cream came out together—not too little, not too much, just a cupful. Francie wished she could ride across the bridge to work and eat in the Automat instead of carrying sandwiches from home.

Even children's books made the Automat a part of their theme. E. L. Konigsburg's *From the Mixed-Up Files of Mrs. Basil E. Frankweiler* has two runaway children hiding out in the Metropolitan Museum of Art and taking their meals at a nearby Automat.

Romance magazines of the thirties, whose heroines often shared the same impecunious fate as their celluloid counterparts, liked to use the Automat as a backdrop. A February 1934 issue of *Serenade* featured a story about a small-town girl who comes to New York City for a career and finds romance. The photo reveals a small clique of women standing in front of a Horn & Hardart steam table while a second group chats at a nearby table. Another story, "Engagement at Five," features a man and woman staring at each other in an Automat. The prose is as awkward as it is purple: "His eyes, and his feet as well, followed her as she carried her tray high through the crowd. A white flame burned in him. If he were ever going to speak to her it must be now."

In 1937, mystery writer Cornell Woolrich wrote a story for *Dime Detective* called "Murder at the Automat." In his story, a man drops into an Automat each night just before closing, puts his nickel in a slot, and pulls out a bologna sandwich. One night, he bites into his sandwich and then drops dead. Who put the cyanide in the bologna sandwich?

Woolrich might have gotten the idea from a real murder mystery that had happened in an Automat nine years before. It started with Harry Jellinor, who, having lost everything in the Depression, decided to commit suicide. Jellinor bought some cyanide and took it to the Automat. He spent what may have been his last nickel on a poppy seed roll. Making a hole in the roll, Jellinor filled it with cyanide and bit into it. After a few minutes, he got up and headed to the men's room, but he never got there. Jellinor dropped dead just outside the door. Meanwhile, Lillian Rosenfeld was sitting at a table on the balcony where she could look down to see who might have left some food. When she saw Jellinor's barely eaten roll, she ran down and finished it off. It took little more than a minute for the cyanide-laced roll to finish Lillian off. Newspapers headlined the mystery of these two deaths in the Automat, and for a few days, the seemingly random poisonings were a threat to Horn & Hardart's existence. When it was learned that Jellinor had committed suicide, Lillian Rosenfeld's financial records were examined: the woman who lived on the street and grubbed other people's food left a bank account worth over twenty-five thousand dollars.

In the 1960s and 1970s, two composers put the Automat to music. P.D.Q. Bach, alias Peter Schickele, composed his *Concerto for Horn & Hardart* in 1965, and David Amram wrote *Horn & Hardart Succotash Blues* in 1973.

The Automat was always a riff that played itself into the souls of the two cities it served. Broadway and Hollywood mined it, artists and writers caught each city's reflections in it. And every time the Automat found itself in print or on celluloid, the restaurant chain that was like no other in the country was reaching a wider audience.

My uncles had a jewelry store just next to a Horn & Hardart on Market Street in Central Philadelphia. I was in Horn & Hardart all the time.

JAMES DARREN

Mashed Turnips

serves 4 to 6

1 medium yellow turnip (about 1 pound),
peeled and cut into 1-inch cubes

1 medium carrot, peeled and cut into 1-inch cubes

1 large Idaho potato, peeled and cut into 1-inch cubes

2 tablespoons unsalted butter

½ medium yellow onion, coarsely chopped
(about ½ cup)

1 teaspoon salt

¼ teaspoon freshly ground white pepper

1 teaspoon sugar

Place the turnip, carrot, potato, and enough water to cover in a 3-quart saucepan. Bring to a boil, then reduce the heat to low and simmer approximately 15 to 20 minutes, or until vegetables are fork-tender; drain.

While the vegetables are cooking, add 1 tablespoon of the butter and onions to a small skillet over medium heat, and sauté about 5 to 8 minutes, until browned and tender.

In an electric mixer, combine the drained vegetables and the sautéed onions. Mix at high speed until smooth, about 2 minutes. (Alternatively, use a ricer or hand-masher.) Add the pepper, sugar, and remaining 1 tablespoon of butter, and blend well.

Rice Pudding

serves 8

2 cups cooked rice

1 quart milk

½ teaspoon salt

¾ cup sugar

3 tablespoons unsalted butter

6 large eggs

1 tablespoon vanilla extract

1½ teaspoons cinnamon

Cook the rice according to package directions.

In a 2-quart saucepan, heat the milk, salt, sugar, and butter over low flame. Cook until the milk is scalded and transfer to 2-quart double boiler. Meanwhile, beat the eggs and vanilla in a medium bowl. Stirring constantly, slowly add the beaten eggs to the double boiler, then the rice, and cook until thickened, about 5 minutes.

Pour the mixture into a 9 × 11 baking pan, sprinkle with the cinnamon, and let stand at room temperature about 30 minutes. Cover and refrigerate until well chilled, about 4 hours.

Opposite: A "Less Work for Mother" retail store in New York City.

When I graduated James Madison High School in 1951, my father gave me
a hundred dollars. I went to Horn & Hardart to eat, and who sat next
to me but the actor Edward Everett Horton.

JIM VALENTI, **Former Director of Loss Prevention for Horn & Hardart**

THE LAST HURRAH

What a relief from New York's hectic pace.

Forty-five cents gets you out of the race.

It's really hip to go back in time.

See 1930 for only a dime.

DAVID AMRAM, "Horn & Hardart Succotash Blues"

In 1950, if you were to ask New Yorkers and Philadelphians to make a list of things they held sacred, close to the top of that list would be Horn & Hardart's five-cent cup of coffee. For nearly a half-century, that's all it took for those dolphin heads to release a generous cupful of Frank Hardart's "gilt-edge" brew, lightened not with milk but with real cream.

Opposite and above: Interior and decorations of the Sixteenth and Chestnut Automat, Philadelphia.

But on November 28, the House That Nickels Built delivered Philadelphians a heavy blow: When customers walked into their favorite Horn & Hardart and scooped up their handful of nickels, it would take two of them to buy the same cup of coffee. The next day, New Yorkers got the same bad news.

For Horn & Hardart, the change was devastating. Even though the price of a telephone call and a ride on a bus or subway had made the nickel-to-dime jump in both cities, there was something psychologically undermining about the coffee move. A year after the increase, New York's Horn & Hardart executives looked at its balance sheet and saw that, for the first time, instead of selling their usual 70 million cups of coffee, they had sold only 45 million cups. Everyone knew it wasn't really about the five cents: The vanished nickel cup of coffee was the straw that broke the tired camel's back, a symptom of a greater problem facing the restaurant chain.

The end of World War II marked a change in where Americans chose to live. Returning GIs moved to the newly built suburbs, putting down payments on the cars that would get them there. Cities lost not only their shine, but much of the emerging middle class. Workers with nine-to-five jobs might catch lunch at an Automat, but at five o'clock they were on their way to their new split-levels and ranch houses.

Labor troubles were also besieging the company. In Philadelphia, attempts by the Teamsters to unionize workers made the news as intimidation and violence were part of the package. Union organizers became so threatening that court injunctions were sought by the company, preventing the organizers from picketing in front of Horn & Hardart facilities. Although attempts at unionization from the mid-fifties into the sixties failed, the company that was once one solid family began to splinter.

Still, the restaurant chain carried on. If Horn & Hardart began to economize on ingredients—using less coffee in the famous brew and replacing cream with milk—they still felt healthy enough to expand. By 1953, Horn & Hardart was boasting 750,000 customers for its combined restaurants and retail shops in both cities. Five years later, the New York company expanded its commissary, which already stretched

an entire block, from Forty-ninth to Fiftieth Streets, between Eleventh and Twelfth Avenues. In 1958, it purchased an additional plot of land across Forty-eighth Street.

In Philadelphia, newspaper items kept informing the public of Horn & Hardart's latest expansions. In 1950, the same year that its coffee jumped to a dime, Horn & Hardart opened its largest Automat-cafeteria and retail shop in the Reading Terminal, located in Philadelphia's Center City. A few months earlier, a building on Fifty-fourth Street and City Line—on the site of the Black Horse Tavern, where George Washington dined—was bought by the company. Before the year was up, an optimistic Horn & Hardart extended its lease on its 1506 Market Street restaurant for another twenty years. Within the next few years, it would bring its restaurants and cafeterias (some of which were being designed by Ralph Bencker) and retail shops to shopping centers in Willow Grove and Manoa.

In 1958, Horn & Hardart reached its earnings peak and opened its eighty-fifth restaurant, in the Castor-Cottman Shopping Center in northeast Philadelphia, touting it as its first suburban cafeteria. In that same year plans were under way to open a Horn & Hardart service restaurant in Delaware. And in 1960, a small article appeared in the *Philadelphia Inquirer* telling of Horn & Hardart's plans to open a few restaurants and retail shops in West Palm Beach, Ft. Lauderdale, and Miami, staffing them with the company's Floridian retirees.

In March 1954, Edwin Daly, president of Horn & Hardart in New York and Philadelphia, included a letter to shareholders with the annual report. He acknowledged the changes the new decade had brought as he tried to project an assuring "we're on top of things" attitude. While people were moving to the suburbs, Horn & Hardart was in hot pursuit. What had not yet been understood by the company was that beyond the great suburban exodus, America's dining tastes were changing. Few people catching lunch at a shopping center wanted to sit down to Salisbury steak, mashed potatoes, and baked beans. And even if a substantial hot meal was on consumers' minds, much of Horn & Hardart's success was due to the consistency of the

Top: Automat in the Airlines
Building, New York City.
Bottom: Picketers in front of the
Philadelphia commissary, 1955.

food—a consistency that resulted from having central commissaries in both cities, each located within a fifteen-mile radius of its Automats and cafeterias. The very concept that had ensured its success had become, in this new decade of mobility, an albatross.

While the company courted the suburban customer, the Automats and cafeterias in both cities began to look run-down and tired. Because of the Depression of the 1930s and the scarcity of men and materials during the war years, nothing had ever been done for these fading grande dames, now in need of face-lifts. In a 1997 interview with Alec Shuldiner for his dissertation, Robert Byrnes, then president of both companies, explained how the companies' fiscal policies worked against the chain:

> *To make alterations to a restaurant cost a fortune, to do it right. The big factor, the biggest factor in the whole thing, was our dividend policy. We had the Philadelphia Company and the Earle family [major stockholders] over there, and they kept demanding dividends, dividends, dividends. As a result we didn't have enough cash when we needed it. We didn't know how to modernize.*

To add to Horn & Hardart's problems, the new office buildings rising in both cities were installing their own subsidized cafeterias. What to do? On January 3, 1955, Horn & Hardart opened a new restaurant across the street from Grand Central Terminal, at 80 East Forty-second Street, in the Air Terminal Building. According to an article in the *Horn & Hardart Herald,* police had to keep the eager crowds from storming the doors to see a new machine in the Automat section. For the first time, patrons could select not just a single item but an entire hot platter. According to the *Herald,* this new unit would do nothing less than "change the eating habits of the New York public who are always in a hurry." The superlatives practically jumped off the page: "Every modern installation known to the restaurant industry is employed by us as well as many that have been developed in the Philadelphia, Pa., Planning

Division, to make this the most modern and efficient layout in the business today."

What management failed to grasp was that the last thing the hurried New Yorker would reach for was that big hot meal. The gimmick, used in only a handful of Automats, failed quickly. Next came cocktails. Breaking a fifty-year policy, in 1961, Philadelphia's Horn & Hardart applied for a liquor license for its Chestnut and Sixteenth Street restaurant, the forty-year-old mother ship that housed its corporate offices. In New York City, 80 East Forty-second Street—the Automat that tried those vended hot-meal platters—got a cocktail lounge, along with an oyster bar and waitresses, and a new name: the Murray Hill. In a few years, Horn & Hardart would transform that same Automat into Nell Gwynn's, a Scottish pub serving ales and such non-Automat food as shepherd's pie. "It will be a real swinging place," said president Tom Hardart. Pennsylvania Station got the Iron Horse Tavern, and Central Park's Zoo had a Horn & Hardart–catered cafeteria. Even in Brooklyn, Horn & Hardart had taken over a spittoon-and-tile-floored old landmark on Court Street and transformed it into a carpeted space serving upscale items like Chicken Le Trianon. Even the "Less Work for Mother" ad campaign was shelved for the less chauvinistic "We're Not Fancy. But We're Good." An odd choice, given the high visibility of its fancy new restaurants.

Frozen food in retail shops, Windowmats (Automat vending machines placed outside for people on the run), Out-O-Mats (takeout

Left: Auction in Philadelphia of the original Automat's fixtures. Opposite: Trucks escorted by police during union negotiations.

meals that were geared to single, upscale New Yorkers), Mobile-Mats (office workers' meals-on-wheels that invaded pocket parks), and Automats on roving flatbed trucks were all attempts to keep up with the times. Horn & Hardart even catered office coffee breaks with its coffee-and-buns carts. And in 1966, Horn & Hardart cosponsored the New York Mets games. For a June 14 game to which company employees were invited, every time a Met hit a home run or stole a base he was rewarded with his weight in Horn & Hardart baked beans. The company also handed out 37,000 one-dollar rain checks to fans, redeemable at any Horn & Hardart restaurant.

Meanwhile, the Automat on the corner of Forty-second Street and Fifth Avenue—the forty-nine-year-old service restaurant that arrived in New York as a market-tester—closed. And in Philadelphia, its venerable Sixteenth and Chestnut building was demolished in 1966, replaced by a 1,300-seat movie theater. "They called it Mr. Horn's favorite restaurant," wrote John F. Morrison in the *Philadelphia Bulletin*. "It was the most beautiful, the finest restaurant in Philadelphia when it opened," said Milena Gates, who was a waitress when it opened in 1925. The following year, another article appeared in the *Bulletin*, this one lamenting the vanishing nickel throwers. "At one time, 120 to 150 were active in this city," wrote Rowland Moriarty. "At last count, only about six were left."

Adding to Horn & Hardart's woes in Philadelphia was the forced closing of its original commissary on South Warnock Street in 1965, when the land was taken over for part of Thomas Jefferson University.

Once, in 1958, when I was in the Chestnut Street cafeteria, the manager caught me kissing my fiancée and threw me out.

WARD CHILDS,
City Archivist,
Philadelphia

"Horn & Hardart went into debt to build the new commissary, expecting to pay back the loan once the new facility went into full production," wrote Sally Alessandroni Downey. According to Downey, the new commissary, in northeast Philadelphia, was problematic from the start: "Horn & Hardart restaurants and retail shops were using only 25 percent of the mammoth plant's production capacity." A plan to place Horn & Hardart products in supermarkets was foiled because supermarkets were unionized and Horn & Hardart wasn't. In 1966, the eighty-year-old company—which had remained profitable through the hard times of the Depression and the manpower and food shortages of World War II—lost money to the tune of $2.4 million. The once-sacrosanct nickel cup of coffee was raised again to fifteen cents as restaurants continued to close.

For Philadelphians, the cruelest blow came in May 1969, when the Horn & Hardart at 818 Chestnut—the original store where Frank Hardart and Joe Horn started it all—was placed on the auction block. Photographs of a mournful manager were in all the newspapers as the door was locked forever. The interior, with its trio of dolphin-headed dispensers and wall of vending machines (the first ones that John Fritsche had remodeled from the original German machine) was carted off to the Smithsonian Institution, in the Museum of American History.

One change was made without much fanfare, yet said more about the company's problems than the jazzy new cocktail bars and themed restaurants or the ascending price of a cup of coffee. In 1966, a new company policy was instituted for a twenty-cent minimum for customers in select Horn & Hardart restaurants in New York City. Even in the sixties, twenty cents didn't count for much, but it was more than most down-and-outers could put together. And it was an enforceable means to keep them out of the Automats. The same types of people who were welcome in the Depression were now asked to leave. "We used to say, 'Come on in, have a glass of water and a toothpick and stay a while,'" said president Bill Curtis in an interview in the mid-sixties. "Which was all right in its day, but no more."

In the thirties and forties, the people living through hard times were all of us. In the economically healthier sixties, those with no money in their pockets were society's fringe, dismissed as bums. Few other people were willing to sit down to lunch or dinner at their table, and these bums were sitting at a lot of Horn & Hardart's tables. "They'd come in, take some hot water and add ketchup and make tomato soup," says Sally Alessandroni Downey, commenting on the Philadelphia restaurants. "They'd stay until the manager threw them out." Even senior citizens, lonely and hungry for some conversation, would nurse their single cups of coffee and begin chatting with people who sat down to a meal at the same table. Before long, the twenty-cent minimum was introduced in Philadelphia.

A new ad campaign underscored the company's desperate need to change its image. Spot television ads and subway posters hammered in the slogan "We're Not Fancy. But We're Good." The hope was to convince quality-conscious New Yorkers that they didn't have to resort to upscale restaurants for good food.

Horn & Hardart wasn't the only chain suffering from lack of customers. In New York, both Schrafft's and Longchamps were feeling deserted. Schrafft's, the bastion of gentility that appealed to women who were more comfortable dining in other women's company, began to lure men with posters showing rough-and-tumble Yankees manager Yogi Berra. Longchamps hired a famous stage designer to zip up its interiors. Neither tactic worked for very long. Society changes, sometimes radically, and rare is the restaurant chain that can survive such change.

Meanwhile, Automats continued to close. In September 1967, a group of elderly women living on their Social Security checks gathered inside the Automat on Seventy-second Street just east of Broadway and sang "Auld Lang Syne" for the end of the thirty-six-year-old restaurant that had sustained them. "Thirty years I'm eating here," said Rose Katz, who depended on the Automat for her social life as well as her sustenance. Time had put Horn & Hardart on the ropes. But the nearly seventy-year-old chain still had a few more rounds to go.

The Final Curtain

Nostalgia is great, but it doesn't pay the bills. Where are all the nostalgia buffs when it comes to buying food?

C. THOMAS GIBBONS,
President, Horn & Hardart Baking Co., Philadelphia, June 1973

In September 1981, Philadelphia's Horn & Hardart Baking Company filed for bankruptcy. It was the company's second filing under Chapter 11, this time to prevent a landlord from taking over its corporate headquarters. Ten years earlier, long after the Automat machines were removed and its waitstaff discontinued, shrinking volume had forced the move. Now, in addition to all of their other problems, overlapping transit strikes had made it almost impossible to deliver food, seriously affecting the company's cash flow. This, in turn, made it difficult for the company to pay its suppliers.

Opposite: 1165 Sixth Avenue, New York City, 1930. Above: 977 Seventh Avenue, New York City, 1933.

Back in New York City, Horn & Hardart was still trying to reinvent its Automats. In 1973, its new president, fifty-one-year-old Fred Guterman, whose expertise was in turning around ailing companies, told the press he was interested in "fun 'n' food" and that he intended to employ plenty of "razzle-dazzle" to lure customers back. Bemoaning the fact that "the golden dawn of sixty years ago has become a sunset of red ink," Guterman pulled out all the stops. Roving hot-dog carts, umbrellas over tables, and employees wearing red-and-white candy-striped shirts and plastic boaters—even artificial waterfalls in some Automats—were all attempts to get some positive attention. At one point, Guterman wanted to install brightly deco-rated booths, reminiscent of a farmer's market, that would hold convenience foods. The front section of the Horn & Hardart at 47 East Fifty-ninth Street was con-verted to a beer garden. Thirteen blocks downtown, customers at Broadway and Forty-sixth Street were serenaded on Wednesday and Thursday nights by gravel-voiced Edna Thayer, "the golden-haired songbird of the Automat," a former vaude-villian whose repertoire included "The Coffee Song" and "The Doughnut Boy." This reinvention reached its comic height in 1973, when customers eating at the Horn & Hardart at 60 East Eighth Street in Greenwich Village were served by waitresses on roller skates.

One thing the New York City Horn & Hardart Company had going for it was real estate. "What people did overlook was that it had phenomenal locations," said Guterman. The company owned land and buildings on sites of fourteen of its thirty-three restaurants, with a book value in 1973 of $7.5 million. Its huge commissary, which had shut down in 1971, fetched $4 million. "I used that real estate as collat-eral to borrow money to buy the mail-order company, Hanover House," said Guterman. Hanover House was a retail and mail-order business with some fifteen catalogs marketing a variety of products. Another thing that Guterman did was to lure the new fast-food chains with Horn & Hardart's prime locations. "I sent wires out to McDonald's, Burger King, and Kentucky Fried Chicken, asking if they would consider." Within days, the president of Burger King showed up and a contract was signed. Horn & Hardart now had exclusive rights to open Burger Kings in Manhattan.

The move drew interest from as far away as Florida, where a thirty-three-year-old former accountant turned Burger King franchisee saw what was happening with Horn & Hardart and decided he'd like to be part of the picture. Barry Florescue, together with partner Donald Schupak, promptly bought 4 percent of the company and let it be known that they planned to run it. "The company would not have survived without him," said Mooney Saltoon, former CEO for Horn & Hardart under Florescue. "Florescue rescued the company from going into final bankruptcy."

In 1977, when Florescue took over, the New York Horn & Hardart was on an express track to financial disaster. Federal and state pension agencies were suing the company over its terminated pension plan, creditors were knocking down the doors, and the American Stock Exchange was threatening to delist the stock. "The Automats were dead by that time and were dead long before that," said Saltoon. Florescue quickly sold most of what was left of the restaurant chain, including the original Times Square Automat, and converted them to Burger Kings. "The Burger Kings were incredibly successful," said David Silver, who was director of marketing for Horn &

Tony Roberts at an Automat celebrity function.

Hardart from 1981 to 1985. "They have a system that enables you to serve lots and lots of people." There were no illusions of trying to keep the Automat alive.

The employees of the few remaining restaurants were not only witnesses to the final death throes, some of them saw nothing wrong with robbing the comatose patient. Jim Valenti, who hired the armored trucks to pick up the money from the restaurants, witnessed a lot of internal theft. His title, director of loss prevention, tells the story. "They had horror stories you wouldn't believe," said Valenti. He recalled one incident: "One girl said to me she went to a Duane Reade pharmacy because she had a toothache. She was making the bank drop, which was $35,000. Somebody hit her over the head, so she never made the deposit. I said to her, 'Well, if your boyfriend's driving around in a red Corvette, I think both of you are going to go to jail.'"

It was a sad state of affairs for a restaurant chain that once prided itself on the sense of family its employees shared. What Florescue did do was to pump money into the Burger King franchises and into the still-healthy mail-order house. By the first quarter of 1978, Horn & Hardart was in the black again, and by year's end it reported a net income of $1.5 million. What happened after that is very contentious. By 1987, *Forbes* magazine, which had done a glowing profile of Florescue in 1983, practically hung him out to dry. In the second profile, *Forbes* accused him of draining the company of six million dollars with a Las Vegas casino he had bought. The magazine didn't stop there, citing his two million dollar purchase of a failed Mark Twain riverboat enterprise and the twelve million dollars of Horn & Hardart money he used to buy Bojangles, a regional chicken-and-biscuit chain that failed. "Schupak and Florescue were milking everything they could get out of Horn & Hardart's success as a Burger King franchisee," said Guterman.

The last decade of Horn & Hardart's life was a sad one. In Philadelphia, only nine restaurants had survived the 1981 bankruptcy. Three years later, just the one restaurant in the Bala Cynwyd Shopping Center on City Avenue—one of Philadelphia's original forty-four—was left standing. Many of the rest had been bulldozed to make way for McDonald's and Gino's Pizzas. "All of my childhood, Horn & Hardart was mostly where my family ate out," said *Philadelphia Inquirer* writer Sally Alessandroni Downey. "Next to my mother's cooking, it was my favorite food."

New York City had one remaining Automat, on the corner of Third Avenue and Forty-second Street. Tucked under a skyscraper, this circa-1958 glass-and-metal box had none of the charm of Ralph Bencker's Art Deco creations. It did have the familiar line of vending machines, but to feed them required 75-cent tokens. The dolphin-

Modernization efforts, clockwise from top left: New York City's last Automat, at Forty-second Street and Third Avenue; 1165 Sixth Avenue in 1965; a new exterior; and a decidedly non–Art Deco interior.

head dispensers no longer got a nightly polish with a toothbrush. And some post-Deco invasions—a salad bar and a counter selling David's cookies—did not allow nostalgia to take root. With the central commissary gone, food was prepared in the kitchen from original recipes. Gone were the Sample Table and the executives who showed up to taste batches of soup and baked beans. Gone were the nickel throwers and the manager whose job it was to make sure each customer left happy.

Because it was the only one left, the city's last Automat became a very popular place to throw parties, including weddings and bar mitzvahs, fetching up to ten thousand dollars for four hours. In the eighties, the company spent money refurbishing its one remaining Automat. "We were promoting it as a venue for parties," says David Silver. For a while, they did a Sunday brunch, but had to stop when not enough people showed up. In 1986, Edith Dickstein, one of the performers on *The Horn & Hardart Children's Hour* during its early radio days, was given a surprise sixtieth birthday party there by her husband. "In each little slot there were hors d'oeuvres," says Dickstein. That same year, the Automat booked twenty-three parties in twenty-three nights. Woody Allen took it over for five hours to shoot a scene for *Radio Days*.

Oddly, with the last Automat still on the respirator, two restaurants popped up that were trading on the very nostalgia the Automats engendered: Dine-O-Mats, fifties-themed chrome-and-neon spots featuring Horn & Hardart dishes. Young men and women who never slipped a couple of nickels into a slot for a slice of pumpkin pie were tutored in the magic of the Automats. The Dine-O-mats were a pleasant albeit ephemeral gimmick that wore thin. And to anyone who knew the Automats when they were a part of the cityscape, the one on Forty-second Street became an out-of-sync, melancholy place whose vitality had long ago been sapped.

On May 12, 1990, Philadelphia lost its last original Automat as the chain filed one final time for bankruptcy. (There was still a Horn & Hardart in Jenkintown, not part of the original, but its days were numbered.) A company spokesman tried to put a positive spin on the event, telling reporters that the trend toward McDonald's and

other fast-food chains had peaked and that it wouldn't be long before "fresh-prepared foods" would again be popular. But everyone knew that for Philadelphians the days of eating at a Horn & Hardart were over.

Nearly a year later, on April 8, 1991, a Tuesday evening, New York City's Automat on Forty-second Street and Third Avenue served its last meal. It got lots of media coverage and its share of private sighs and lamentations bemoaning the end of the good old days. And then it was over. Horn & Hardart, the restaurant chain that had served the city for eight decades, imprinting itself as much on a time as it did on the lives of those who lived it, was a memory.

Like many institutions that outlive their time, Horn & Hardart went out with a whimper. Few noticed the last closings in New York and Philadelphia. People had changed. The cities were no longer an easy mix of blue-collar and white-collar workers. Newt Disney, a man who chose to share his memories of a trip to Horn & Hardart in Philadelphia with us, summed it up: "I'd take my children to the Ice Follies or to see Wanamaker's Christmas display, and we'd end the day at the Automat, joining other families eating there. Sitting at your table might be a group of attorneys or stockbrokers, a policeman, a couple of young Catholic high-school girls, or a homeless person. That was Horn & Hardart."

It was the rarest phenomenon of the twentieth century: Communism that worked and capitalism that worked.

STEVE STOLLMAN,
theautomat.com

Tapioca Pudding

serves 8

½ cup large pearl tapioca

3 cups milk

½ cup sugar

½ teaspoon salt

1 large egg, beaten

1½ teaspoons vanilla extract

¼ teaspoon nutmeg

In a 2-quart double boiler, soak the tapioca in 3 cups of water overnight in the refrigerator.

Drain the water. Add the milk, sugar, salt, and egg to the tapioca in the double boiler. Cook over medium-low heat, stirring continuously, until the mixture is thickened and the tapioca pearls are translucent, about 40 minutes. Remove from the heat and stir in the vanilla and nutmeg. Pour into 8 individual cups and let stand at room temperature about 20 minutes. Cover and refrigerate until chilled, about 2 hours.

Mashed Sweet Potatoes

serves 6

4 medium sweet potatoes (about 2 pounds), peeled

4 tablespoons (½ stick) unsalted butter

¼ cup sugar

1 teaspoon salt

¼ teaspoon freshly ground white pepper

¼ cup milk, room temperature

In a 3-quart saucepan over high heat, heat the potatoes and enough water to cover them to boiling. Reduce the heat to low and simmer approximately 30 to 40 minutes, or until fork-tender. Drain in a colander and allow the potatoes to sit for 2 minutes, to dry completely.

In an electric mixer at low speed, blend potatoes, butter, sugar, salt, and pepper for about 3 minutes, until the potatoes are completely broken up. Add the milk gradually while whipping. Whip at high speed for 1 to 2 minutes, until the potatoes are smooth.

Acknowledgments

So many people gave of their memories that we have chosen to thank them collectively. Several people provided immeasurable help, including Sally Alesandroni Downey and Paul Downey, who generously opened their files and their memories, and pointed us in the right direction; the late Bill Curtis, who tirelessly shared his memories; and especially Steve Stollman, who put us in touch with valuable resources, including each other. The extensive collection of the late Robert F. Byrnes, a Horn & Hardart employee for sixty-three years, provided invaluable materials, John Faitakes shared his stories and memorabilia, and Edith Dickstein shared not only her memories of *The Children's Hour* but also her photographs. Thanks to Rosemary Hardart Dobbin for her basement treasures, Thomas Hardart Jr., Paul Hardart, Anne Hardart, Marcy Hardart and Matt Wickline, Donald Fowley and Andy Romeo, Gus Hardart, Margot Curran, Matthew Goldstein, Alan Zaretsky, Eileen Kowal, Birdie Brady, Dorra Blacker, and Norma Taylor. At the New York Public Library, Mimi Bowling and her staff, and Tom Lisanti, manager, Photographic Services & Permissions. Others contributed photographs to the project. In Philadelphia, Bruce Laverty at The Athenaeum of Philadelphia, Susan Drysdale at the Atwater Kent Museum, Brenda Wright at Urban Archives, Temple University Libraries, and Joe Benford at The Free Library of Philadelphia. In New York, Allen Reuben of Culver Pictures, Ron Mandelbaum at Photofest, Klaus Gugelberger at the *New York Daily News*. Eileen Morales at the Museum of the City of New York, and Carrie Cole and David Shayt at the Smithsonian Institution. A special thanks to Bill Curtis Jr., Jonathan Gell, Roslyn Willet, Clint Bloom, Ray Messina, Rene Block, Nikki Krajik, and Louise Drevers, and Dr. Esther Chackes for her vision. Alec Tristin Shuldiner generously provided his dissertation. We are especially grateful to Nancy Hardart for her fact-finding and endless support; Bill Diehl, our enthusiastic supporter and magic button to the celebrities in this book; JillEllyn Riley, who gave practical advice; and our editor, Chris Pavone, whose wry sense of humor was a welcome riff throughout the usually enjoyable and sometimes maddening process of finishing a book. The recipes in this book were adapted and tested by Maria Baldo, a gifted nutritionist and a true friend.

Bibliography

Barrett, Mary Ellin. *Irving Berlin: A Daughter's Memoir* (New York: Simon & Schuster, 1994).

Konigsburg, E. L. *From the Mixed-Up Files of Mrs. Basil E. Frankweiler* (New York: Atheneum, 1967).

Langdon, Philip. *Orange Roofs, Golden Arches: The Architecture of American Chain Restaurants* (New York: Alfred A. Knopf, 1986).

Morand, Paul. *New York* (New York: Henry Holt and Co., 1930).

Shuldiner, Alec Tristin. *Trapped Behind the Automat: Technological Systems and the American Restaurant, 1902–1991* (Cornell University, 2001).

Smith, Betty. *A Tree Grows in Brooklyn* (New York: Harper & Row Perennial, 1968; 1943).

Woolrich, Cornell. *Murder at the Automat* (New York: The Reader's Digest Association, Inc., 1990) by special arrangement with the Bowling Green State University Popular Press, 1983. First published in 1937 in *Dime Detective,* reprinted in *Nightwebs* (New York: Harper & Row, 1971).

Sources

In addition to interviews with those individuals who remember Horn & Hardart and the Automats and the people who worked in them, a good deal of information came from the extensive collection—the scrapbooks of newspaper clippings, correspondence and photographs—of the late Robert Byrnes, which makes up the Robert Byrnes Collection of Automat Memorabilia at the New York Public Library.

Page 34. **"not just machinery but machinery with splendor"** Philip Langdon, *Orange Roofs, Golden Arches: The Architecture of American Chain Restaurants, 1902–1991.* New York: Alfred A. Knopf, 1986, pp. 16–17.

Page 38. **"Customers could choose not only . . ."** Alec Tristin Shuldiner, *Trapped Behind the Automat: Technological Systems and the American Restaurant, 1902–1991.* New York: Cornell University, 2001, p. 52.

Page 42. **"Perhaps the finest Art Deco restaurant exterior . . ."** Philip Langdon, *Orange Roofs, Golden Arches: The Architecture of American Chain Restaurants, 1902–1991.* New York: Alfred A. Knopf, 1986, p. 22.

Page 58. **"New York in those days had only . . ."** Robert F. Byrnes, *New York Times.* 1982.

Page 71. **"Into the forties, I maintained . . ."** Neil Simon, "The Automat," *New York* magazine. December 21–28, 1987.

Page 76. **"I was originally hired as a machineman . . ."** Sam Stitch, *Horn & Hardart Herald.* October 1953, Vol. No. 3.

Page 78. **"Marriages between H & H employees were common . . ."** Sally Alesandroni Downey, "Of Love and the Automat," *Philadelphia Inquirer.* April 29, 1984, p. 12.

Page 78. **"Short of committing a felony . . ."** Jack Alexander, "The Restaurant That Nickels Built." *Saturday Evening Post.* December 18, 1954, p. 57.

Page 86. **"They wanted me to do a short commercial . . ."** Marjorie Farnsworth, "The Prideful Poor of South Philadelphia," *Cosmopolitan,* March 1963, pp. 12–17.

Page 86. **"We don't want to put a lot of squeaky brats on the air."** *Time,* April 26, 1943, pp. 42–44.

Page 91. **"The Brozas gave me my first chance . . ."** Marjorie Farnsworth, "The Prideful Poor of South Philadelphia," *Cosmopolitan,* March 1963, pp. 12–17.

Page 96. **"Maybe he walked me up Sixth Avenue . . ."** Mary Ellin Barrett, *Irving Berlin: A Daughter's Memoir,* New York: Simon & Schuster, 1994, p. 91.

Page 101. **"They are delightful, these bars . . ."** Paul Morand, *New York,* New York: Henry Holt and Company, 1930, p. 60.

Page 102. **"And Neely ate in a restaurant."** Betty Smith, *A Tree Grows in Brooklyn,* New York: Harper & Row Perennial, 1968; 1943, p. 323.

Page 102. **"His eyes, and his feet as well . . ."** "Engagement at Five," short story appearing in unknown romance magazine. Robert Byrnes Collection of Automat Memorabilia, *Scrapbook: 1926–1936.*

Page 111. **"To make alterations to a restaurant . . ."** Alec Tristin Shuldiner, *Trapped Behind the Automat: Technological Systems and the American Restaurant, 1902–1991,* 2001, p. 175.

Page 112. **"It will be a real swinging place."** Tom Hardart, "Only Human" column by Sidney Fields, newspaper unknown.

Page 113. **"They called it Mr. Horn's favorite restaurant."** John F. Morrison, *The Philadelphia Bulletin,* March 7, 1966.

Page 113. **"Horn and Hardart went into debt . . ."** Sally Alessandroni Downey, "Of Love and the Automat," *Inquirer Magazine,* April 29, 1984.

Page 115. **"Thirty years I'm eating here . . ."** "Closing of Automat on 72nd Street Ends an Era for Elderly," *New York Times,* September 18, 1967.

Page 117. **"Nostalgia is great, but . . ."** C. Thomas Gibbons, president, Horn & Hardart Baking Co., Philadelphia *Daily News,* June 28, 1973.

Index

Credits

All photographs and illustrations courtesy of the Hardart Family, except the following, used by permission: Pages 2, 32, 106, 107, 110 (bottom): Athenaeum of Philadelphia; page 8: Edward Hopper (American, 1882–1967), *Automat,* 1927; Oil on Canvas; 29⅛ × 36 inches; 71.4 × 91.4 cm; Des Moines Art Center Permanent Collections; Purchased with funds from the Edmundson Art Foundation, Inc., 1958.2; Photo Credit: Michael Tropea, Chicago; page 10: The Fireman Group Café Concepts; page 15: Smithsonian Institution National Museum of History; pages 16, 55, 71 (top), 110 (top), 112, 113: Temple University Libraries; pages 20, 56: Culver Pictures, Inc.; pages 23, 31 (top left, top right, bottom right), 36, 40, 43, 44, 46 (right), 48, 49, 53 (top), 57, 58, 66, 71 (bottom left and right), 72, 77, 89 (bottom right), 95, 105, 116, 117, 121: Robert F. Byrnes Collection of Automat Memorabilia, 1912–1990s, New York Public Library; pages 34, 42, 64, 82: The Museum of the City of New York; pages 35 (bottom left), 94, 96, 97, 98 (top left, bottom left, bottom right), 99 (top right, bottom right): Photofest; page 53 (bottom right): Free Library of Philadelphia; page 60 (top left): Bettman/CORBIS; page 67: *The New Yorker;* pages 84, 89 (top), 92: The Atwater Kent Museum; pages 85, 89 (bottom left), 90: Edith Dickstein; page 98 (top right): *Time;* pages 99 (top left), 100: *New York Daily News;* page 101: *Seventeen;* page 119: Christina Krupka/D'Arlene Studios.

Hot Vegetables

Buttered Cabbage
Harvard Beets
Whipped Potatoes
Green Peas

Health Salad
Home Fried Potatoes
Buttered Rice
Baked Beans ... 40
Spaghetti ... 45

Buttered Carrots
Buttered String Beans
French Fried Potatoes

Sandwiches

DOUBLE DECKERS on Toast
Tuna Fish Salad and Tomato
Chicken Salad and Sliced Tongue

Special Sandwich Omelettes

Sliced Chicken on Toast (All White Meat) ... 55
De Luxe Ham and Lettuce ... 40 ... Sardines and Lettuce ... 40
De Luxe Tongue and Lettuce ... 40
Bacon, Tomato and Lettuce ... 30 ... Chicken Salad ... 30

Salads

Tuna Fish Salad, Tomato, Egg and Lettuce ... 50
Ham, Potato Salad, Tomato, Lettuce ... 45
Chicken Salad, Tomato, Lettuce ... 55
Ham, Tongue, Health Salad, Tomato, Lettuce ... 55

Beverages

Horn and Hardart Grill Edge Coffee ... 10
Tea, Horn and Hardart Blend or Orange-Pekoe ... 10
Hot Chocolate ... 20 ... with Whipped Cream
Milk (Glass) ... 10 ... Postum ... 10
Buttermilk (Bottle) ... 15 ... Chocolate or Vanilla Malted Milk ... 30
Iced Cold Coca Cola (Glass) ... 10 ... Chocolate Float ... 25